A VIEW FROM BELOW

A VIEW FROM BELOW

RYAN RAMSEY

ISBNs
Paperback: 978-1-80541-396-7
eBook: 978-1-80541-397-4
Hardcover: 978-1-80541-398-1

CONTENTS

INTRODUCTION

All leaders are readers, Harry S. Truman said. But when there are so many leadership books out there to read, how do you know which is right? And how do you know it comes from a source you can trust? Drawn from a course renowned for the calibre of leaders it produces and written by someone who both took and taught it, this book translates its leadership lessons for the business world.

The British Royal Navy's Submarine Command Course is the most demanding leadership course in the world — without exception. Nicknamed the 'Perisher' because of its toughness, it's the envy of other submarine forces, admired by those organisations who know what it is, hated by those who fail and idolised by those who pass. Since its inception in 1917, only around 1,000 officers have passed the course. Those who fail — perish. They can never serve on a submarine again. Every year, the Navy spends millions of pounds running the six-month course, despite knowing that only four out of the six candidates are likely to make it through. Why? Because commanding a submarine is believed to be the toughest and most important job in the military.

Only one man decides whether a Perisher student passes or fails: the course tutor, known simply as 'Teacher'. Hand-picked from the Navy's best, most-experienced commanding officers, being chosen as 'Teacher' is an honour granted to few. From 2012 to 2014 I was Teacher and for me, it was a great way to give back to the submarine service.

A submarine warfare officer for over 20 years, serving with three different navies and spending over 6500 days at sea, my greatest privilege was to command HMS *Turbulent*, a nuclear-powered attack submarine.[1] I use the word *command* because that is the word the

---

[1] HMS Turbulent is the second Royal Navy submarine to bear the name. The first HMS Turbulent was a Triton Class submarine launched in 1941 which served during WW2 until 1943 when she was sunk by a mine close to the Maddalena Archipelago off Sardinia.

military uses, however, the reality was I served. I served my team by providing personal support, leadership and decision-making.

Command is a privileged position. It's a position earned not purely by being selected and successfully completing Perisher, it's earned once you are onboard a submarine, leading your team. Submarine Command has always been and will always be about people. It is people who operate the complex submarine. It is people who go through emotional cycles and it is people who succeed and fail. Leadership should be about ensuring success as a team, enabling men and women to learn their individual limits and how to operate within them. And finally, as a team, learn to depend on each other because they want to and not because they have to.

Before HMS *Turbulent*, I'd been meticulous about collecting information and practising everything I could to lead well immediately. I had a baseline of over 200 commanders I'd either served, taught or observed, to analyse. I learned there are common trends. There are natural leaders — without a doubt — and there are those who can't lead (which is alright as long as they're not in a leadership position).

I also learned that you must not for a moment believe the leader is the most powerful person; they are not. Power — if that's important to you — rests with the follower. Because the most important thing must always be the team. It wasn't for me to decide that my style, ethics and leadership style were correct. It was for those who chose to follow. For me, 'servant leadership' worked through what was a very long and varied command. I served my team and their families.

Despite the fact so few have experienced it, submarine command has so much to give back to the rest of society about leadership and decision-making. Leadership is a privileged position. It's one you have to earn, not only by selection and successful completion of courses but, most importantly, once you are on board and leading your team. Your team, their families, half a billion pounds worth of military hardware, a nuclear reactor, weapons, operating alone in a void less explored than space, mission orders that are broad but allow you to plan and execute without recourse to others, making decisions with a political consequence, decisions with a consequence to life — that it is the responsibility of submarine command in the 21st Century.

Since leaving the Navy, during my subsequent civilian career, I've seen first-hand how the leadership lessons Perisher teaches transcend the submarine service and translate into the business world. Sharing these lessons and taking that leadership message to a wider audience is a way to give back what I know to everyone.

Perisher has evolved over the years. Not just because submarine technology has advanced, but because the tactics required to fight in differing warfare landscapes have changed over time. However, the values underpinning the course remain the same: leadership and decision-making. It's as simple as that.

The course I taught was different from my predecessor's and needed to be; the warfare domain was transitioning rapidly. Automation, changing priorities for warfighting, resurgent Russia, and counterterrorism, all of these had an effect on the course I was to deliver.

Perisher's structure is explained in more detail in the first chapter of this book, but in general terms, it begins by setting the context (our history, our political landscape, the strategic landscape, the operational landscape). This is followed by nine weeks in a variety of simulators conducting safety and operations training, then four weeks at sea (two weeks training, and two weeks assessment). When you have completed all that — and if you've passed — you conduct four weeks of administrative updates (people, engineering, visits to various agencies you will interact with during your time as Executive Officer (XO) and a Commanding Officer (CO).

A submarine is the most complex military hardware the Navy owns, capable of landing lethal strikes via torpedo or missile. Its role is to deliver violence to the enemy and as Teacher, my job was to provide a crew with the best possible captain to do this. It wasn't just fighters I was after, though, it was leaders. Because when you're in command of a submarine, the buck stops with you. You alone are responsible for the lives of over 130 people. It's crucial your crew follows you because they want to. Not because they have to.

Over the next nine chapters, I'll share with you the leadership lessons from the sea phase of the Perisher course as I taught it. This is the phase where, after two weeks of training, students' leadership skills are scrutinised while they are put to the test at sea under extreme pressure. Interspersed with real-life Perisher scenarios,[2] each chapter explores an element integral to strong leadership and relates these to situations you're likely to encounter in the business world.

After explaining a little about the history of Perisher— what it is, who gets selected for it, why it's so difficult, and the challenges of submarine command — the first half of the book then deals with knowledge: of yourself; your team; and your enemy. In Chapter Two, we'll explore why you want to lead, what sacrifices you're prepared to make and how you learn your personal limits — mental and physical — in order to know yourself. Chapter Three discusses the importance of knowing your team so you understand when dynamics change and how to inspire them. Equally important, is knowing your enemy. Chapter Four explains why good leaders are prepared leaders — you can't go against an enemy or potential enemy without understanding them and knowing what motivates them.

In the second half of the book, we'll cover topics from planning, to leading out of context and how to challenge effectively. Chapter Five explains how to make your planning efficient to ensure sustainable performance, while Chapter Six's focus is on the art of decision-making. You'll discover how to assess risk, how much information is enough to make a decision; how to judge the last safe moment to make a decision; how to justify your decisions and how you learn to have the moral courage decision-making requires.

Chapter Seven reveals my simple leadership model. It covers what you should do, what you should avoid, how to influence your team

---

[2] The Perisher scenarios used in this book are all taken from my time as Teacher. However, they are not in strict chronological order.

with integrity and how to lead out of context, as well as how you empower yet retain the ability to intervene at the right time. Chapter Eight examines a little taught skill: how to challenge effectively. You'll learn when to lead, when to be consiglieri, and how to follow. In the final chapter we'll explore what taking command involves, especially if you're taking over from someone who is well-liked or, at the other extreme, someone who has battered your new team. Each requires a different approach. As well as mastering these, you'll find out how to change the culture subtly to deliver results.

Those of you who are already accomplished leaders may find snippets throughout the book useful. For those of you who are early on in your leadership journey or just starting out, it will give you some ideas about what to concentrate on. This is important. Because although organisations provide leadership training, you'll get much more out of a training course if you know what you want to achieve from it.

Reading this book will not only make you a better leader, you'll understand more about yourself. But before we get started, there are some underpinning principles we as leaders should remember:

- Leaders are an overhead unless they get the best from their team.
- Servant leaders have the humility and courage to learn from those who have less power.
- Create a culture of continual learning — it's brilliant. Learn and share so others can too.
- Be humble — enjoy humility.
- Never enter anything you can't get out of.
- Never make it about you — the moment you do that, you lose — morally, ethically, and generally.
- Create your own leadership values — what's important to you, not the company. Live by them.

Enjoy the journey.

THE JOURNEY TO TRIUMPH

The Scottish coast can be a brutal place but it can also be beautiful and the weather plays a large part in this. Departing to sea from Faslane Naval Base, the home of the Submarine Service, you travel through the Garloch, the Rhu Narrows and down towards the Isle of Arran. The landscape is incredible: varying from high hills to individual isolated dwellings to small towns all on the coast. If you're on the bridge of a surfaced submarine, you can take some of this in, even if you're navigating or a lookout. Down below it's always far busier. The Control Room will be filled with extra crew in order to deal with navigating these restricted waters safely. Things can go wrong very quickly, so focused attention is vital.

But at this point, you're not on a submarine, you're on a 'tender', the SD Eva, a medium size transport boat taking you, five other student captains and Teacher to the host submarine, *Triumph*. This is the start of the sea phase of Perisher and the final part of nearly six months of training and a lifetime journey to get to this point. You and the other student captains are all equally apprehensive. It's why you're all making conversation unnecessarily. You've built bonds with each other during the previous four months, but you know not all of you will pass. It's a real dilemma – you want everyone to succeed, but not everyone can, and you don't want to be the person that couldn't. Self-doubt is a killer, but so is over-confidence and arrogance.

The tender turns West out of the Rhu Narrows heading outbound. In 25 minutes, you will reach the submarine and it begins.

Time. The one thing you never seem to have enough of. This is one of the first lessons of leadership: use time wisely. You've known which submarine you are going to be on board for the sea phase of the course for several months now and have occasionally been in touch with the Executive Officer (XO – Second in Command).

While all submarines are similar, they're never identical. The major difference is always the crew and how they work together.

The submarine you'll be joining has just completed a patrol and is now 'hosting' Perisher. The crew you're about to operate with will be professional and courteous, but they will already have gelled. They know you're coming, how stressful the course is, and how much pressure you and they will be under. You'll know some people from previous submarines you've served on, but you won't know everyone and there will be much to do to integrate rapidly.

SD Eva passes Brodick Bay and Teacher brings the student captains together. Standing on the deck of EVA in sea-going uniforms and life jackets, you 'huddle'. Teacher looks each of you in the eye.

"Okay, we're nearly there. You set the tone from the start. Everything you've done so far now enables you to demonstrate you've got what it takes. As I've said before, some of this will be training, but a lot is assessment. I wish you all the best."

Teacher heads up to the bridge. He'll be going to speak to the submarine on VHF radio, thank the captain of SD Eva and check in with HQ (Northwood).

There's little small talk now between the students, you're all thinking the same thing. Have you done enough preparation, and fulfilled everything Teacher asked you to do with the course structure? Maybe, maybe not, but you convince yourself you have — that way failure will be justified. You also tell yourself there's way you'll fail. No doubt. Those who doubt, fail.

You think about your family, knowing you won't have time to think about them for the rest of the course. You have another famialso know you have a family you spend way more time with – the submarine family. You know that one day, you'll have to reconcile this – but now is not about that – you need to focus.

Looking out again, you see you're now heading down the Clyde. The boat is fast. There's Rothesay, now you're heading to the Cumbrae Gap. That gap, less than 200 metres wide, has seen many a submarine go through dived at depth. It's a crazy experience and you only remember it from being a navigator — how tense it was, how much risk was involved, how engaged you were. But the responsibility was always with the Captain, and he just looked calm. You know at some point, you'll be involved in doing it again, you just don't know whether you'll be the Duty Captain for it.

Scotland is renowned for having four seasons in one day, so it's no surprise the weather is worsening. So are your nerves. First impressions…you must make the right first impression. Despite Teacher telling you it doesn't always help, it can't hurt. So many things are running around your head. Your only previous experience of Perisher before this was as a junior officer when you were part of the crew observing the student captains being put through their paces. Now it's your turn. You've trained for four months to get to this point. You need to stop remembering that and get control of yourself. But the pressure you're putting on yourself…you can't control it even though you know you should and that's creating more pressure. You're feeling more and more nervous.

There she is. *HMS Triumph* now comes into view. Even if you see them regularly, submarines always look imposing and *Triumph's* a mean beast: 5200 tonnes of war-fighting capability. The setting just adds gravitas. The hills, the slanting rain, the darkening sky and low-hanging clouds are turning what's picture-postcard scenery on a sunny day, to something more sinister and ominous-looking. It changes the whole experience. You'll want to minimise the time on deck because the wind is now picking up and the rain is constant, sometimes horizontal.

Teacher goes out on deck and you follow, lining up facing the submarine as the SD Eva crew get ready to go alongside the submarine. It's close now. As you draw nearer, looking directly at the top of the fin you can see the XO, Navigator and Radio Operator on the bridge. The XO is leaning over looking at the casing (deck) where the sailors known as the casing party are standing, ready to bring you on board.

The Captain is also standing on the casing. As SD Eva gets closer, Teacher shouts, "Morning, Captain".

"Morning, Teacher," the Captain shouts back. Both of them somehow managing to make themselves heard over the noise of the tender's engine.

As the gangway lowers you see a junior officer preparing to cross. He'll be coming to give you all a safety brief. You've heard it so many times — in fact you've given it yourself in the past — which is why you know it's important you listen, for two reasons. The first is because something may have changed. The second is because his focus is ensuring your safety during the transfer from tender to submarine. Dismiss his effort and you disrespect him. So you listen intently and at the end of the briefing when he catches your eye you give him a smile and nod to acknowledge he's done well.

Teacher crosses the gangway first and, true to centuries-old, naval tradition, he's piped on board. He salutes and climbs down the main access hatch. Next across is the senior student, and then it's your turn. Nuclear power means the only noise you can hear is SD Eva's engine. But you're getting closer to the world you love.

Chapter 1

Perisher

'It's easy, once you have experienced it, to understand how Perisher has acquired its coating of legend. It's both a training and an initiation rite, all performed in front of an entire crew. Those who pass feel they are a special breed.'

Peter Hennessy & James Jinks, *The Silent Deep*.

According to author Tom Clancy, Royal Navy submarine commanders are the most feared in the world. "Note that I use the word 'fear'," says Clancy. "Not just respect. Not just awe. But real fear at what a British submarine, with one of their superbly qualified captains at the helm, might be capable of doing."

To qualify as submarine captain an officer of the Royal Navy must first pass Perisher, the world's toughest command course — a course so revered that even the US Navy puts its best officers through it. Originally named the Periscope School when it was established in September 1917, the Royal Navy Submarine Command Course (SMCC) as it's now formally known, earned its 'Perisher' nickname in the 1930s. A conflation of 'Periscope' and 'School', the moniker also has a darker inference. Failing means the 'perishing' of your submarine career; your underwater service in the Navy is over.

It's a big deal even to be put forward for Perisher and the selection process is rigorous. Only four to six officers (usually Lieutenants or Lieutenant Commanders) are accepted for each 18-week course. There are up to two courses a year aiming to produce between five and six Submarine Command Qualified Officers in total.

A Perisher candidate has about 10-12 years of experience as a submariner, most of which will have been at sea. They are warfare officers, they are focused, they want to be selected, and they want to be successful. Why? To earn the ultimate prize. To serve a team as a submarine captain: to *command*.

No two candidates will have the same mix of skills and characteristics but according to former Teacher, Martin Macpherson, the most successful Commanding Officers (COs) all share certain qualities:

> "All accepted responsibility eagerly and were self-confident. They were strong-willed, tenacious and determined; they were brave; and they possessed great physical and mental stamina. They all cared passionately for their ships' companies, had a strong sense of humour and many were surprisingly modest. Their professional experience and training had developed quick calculating brains, the ability to delegate, presence, and a 'good periscope eye'[3] — able to react instinctively without losing sight of the bigger picture developing on the surface."

Perisher exists to assess these qualities and to teach leadership. It's a unique pathway to a unique position. Compared to other commanding roles in the navy, its underwater environment and isolation make submarine command an autonomous one; a 'one-man show'.

Captain Herman de Groot, RNLN, Former Head of the Dutch Submarine Service explains it like this:

> "The submarine CO takes his weapon system all over the globe and is the epitome of mission command. His reason for

---

[3] Martin MacPherson, Perisher: the making of a Submarine Commander in *100 Years of the Trade*, (CDISS, 2001).

being is to solve things on his own without the consultation options other commanders have. Although the submarine CO cannot do a thing without his crew, all actions go through him. He is the true Spider-Man in the middle of his web".[4]

How Perisher evolved

Before World War I, submarine command training was passed from one commander to the next. During the war, the mortality rate was so high it often meant there was no one to pass on this knowledge. As officers inexperienced in periscope use and without specialist attack training were more likely to make mistakes — leading to loss of life as well as submarines — Commodore Sydney Hall requested Admiralty approval to establish the School. And on 6 October 1917, 23-year-old Lieutenant John Mundell was the first officer to graduate.

In 1917, just five days of periscope attack training was required before an officer could be appointed to command a submarine. By 2017, Perisher took five months. During that time, the course evolved in order to adapt to new types of warfare (the Cold War, for example) and keep up with advances in technology as well as the introduction of nuclear power and new weapons systems.

But while Perisher's format may have altered throughout the decades and its syllabus size has grown, its purpose remains the same. To pass, you must show you can operate a submarine safely, effectively and aggressively in a hostile environment. To prove this, you will complete a series of tactical tests under close scrutiny. These run the gamut of any tactical scenario you might expect to experience as a Submarine Commander and include everything from attacking an enemy to gathering intelligence and delivering special forces.

---

[4] Herman de Groot quoted in David Parry, *Perisher: 100 Years of the Submarine Command Course*, The Choir Press, 2022, p.12.

Perisher in the 21st Century

The first phase of Perisher takes place ashore and starts with four weeks of safety training in submarine simulators. This develops your ability to apply safety rules when you're operating a submarine at periscope depth (PD) in close proximity to a number of aggressive warships. This submarine safety training, which will teach you to appreciate the importance of accuracy and honesty, is followed by a week's training at sea with what the Navy calls 'live assets' (real people operating real systems).

Next comes Mission Training — six weeks of tactical training in simulators designed to test your professional knowledge, tactical acumen, and willingness to take calculated military risks. It's achieved through the use of progressive and challenging contemporary scenarios incorporating national missions, NATO missions, fire control training, use of manoeuvring room, ship control and damage control (DC) trainers. It culminates in a week's mission rehearsal to prepare you for sea-phase scenarios. Then, if — and only if — Teacher decides your practical skills are good enough, you will proceed to the sea phase.

The sea phase of Perisher takes four weeks. The most gruelling and intense part of the course it's designed to test your leadership and management skills to the full. It's much more than a test of your practical skills, though. What's really being examined here are your leadership qualities; whether you have what it takes to command under extreme pressure in stressful situations. To test this, you and the other students take turns as Duty Captain and are closely scrutinised during battle scenarios where the lives of 130 crew are in your hands.

Most of your time will be spent in the Control Room, which sits pretty centrally in the submarine, beneath the fin (housing the masts). Firstly, you're put through your paces during intense, 'eyes-only' sessions. No matter how experienced you are as a submarine officer (and Perisher candidates all have distinguished naval careers behind them) there's nothing like taking command of a nuclear submarine and its crew. You may find it easy to cope with one or two frigates in the simulator. At sea, it's completely different.

Playing chicken with charging warships means continuously tracking their range using speedy mental arithmetic, making split-second calculations and decisions under intense pressure. Get your sums wrong and you could put the submarine and crew in danger. A serious mistake could cause a collision which may result in casualties — it has been known to happen, historically.

There'll be the weather to factor in too. (Bad weather and poor visibility make ranging harder but sunny skies can be problematic too — bright sunlight will glint off the periscope as soon as it breaks the surface). Teacher will also up the ante, introducing frigates and helicopters designed to seek out and destroy submarines, and throwing 'enemy' submarines and civilian vessels into the mix just to see how you cope. As well as demonstrating your leadership skills while gathering intelligence, you'll also need to prove to Teacher, your ability to plan, command and execute the covert launch and release of Special Forces.

If you manage to get through this first sea phase of Perisher, the course then gets harder. So far, you'll have been dodging the enemy in deep seas. Next, you must prove you can conduct reconnaissance, launch and recover specialist forces and deliver land strikes in perilously shallow water without running aground.

For example, your mission may be to take periscope pictures without being detected while avoiding obstacles not just to your left, right, fore, and aft, but above and below you. That requires thinking in 3-D as you manoeuvre an 86-metre-long submarine in seas as shallow as 45 metres. As well as the very real danger of running aground, you'll be dealing with hostile warships and helicopters all with approval to attack.

During any mission, Teacher will wind up the pressure - he needs to know your limits and whether they're sufficient to command. The pressure is not solely from outside forces, but from inside amongst your crew. When 130 people spend months at sea together in a submarine tensions can mount and tempers flare without warning. You may have to cope with the disruption caused by a noisy crew member in the Control Room, during an intense operation. Or a distraction caused by two officers struggling over who's responsible for doing what, and when. How you deal with the issue in your team — whatever it may be — and regain control of the situation is what counts.

You won't just come under Teacher's watchful eye during the sea phase of Perisher either. Naval VIPs are brought on to the submarine to pass on their wisdom and provide interference. Your decisions will be questioned and you'll need to justify your actions — and dealing with VIPs brings a separate intensity that's difficult to describe. You want your decision to be right, to be seen to be in control even when you might not be. That introduces decision risk, which you need to manage.

As a large part of being a submarine commander involves admin and managerial tasks you can expect these skills to be put under the microscope too, by making captain's rounds and inspecting the boat, making sure everything is clean, well-stowed and secured. This also creates an opportunity for you to get to speak to the crew in different departments. Teacher will be monitoring the way you interact with your team on a regular basis as well as how you motivate, inspire and encourage them under pressure in stressful conditions.

Hunting for other submarines and weapons firing (of virtual torpedoes) come next. You'll be scrutinised to see if you can hold your own against other, highly experienced submarine commanders in a war scenario with threats coming from aircraft above the surface too.

If you successfully pass that phase of the course, you'll enter the final stages: a simulated war between two fictional countries involving around 5,000 personnel. Your mission, to survey and attack surface targets. But before Teacher decides who will, or won't finish the course, you'll face the ultimate challenge in the captain's chair, an inshore mission involving really difficult decisions in a time deficit environment. During this task, you must prove you can adapt if your superiors change orders at the last minute too.

Finally, having been pushed to the limit, your weaknesses exposed and your mind played with, it's decision time. Have you passed or failed?

From the moment you arrive at the submarine to start the sea phase of Perisher, you know you're on trial. You also know you could fail the course at any time. However, making a mistake during the sea phase doesn't mean you'll automatically fail as long as you recognise your mistake and correct it without endangering the lives of your crew and the submarine. If you don't pass it won't be because you lack experience or qualifications, it will be because you're just not cut out for submarine command. Perisher's low pass rate and its renowned toughness mean there's no stigma attached to failure. Your days as a submariner will be over but you'll be advised where your future career in the Navy lies.

If you're successful, you'll hear the words "Congratulations, Captain" and will be offered a glass of champagne. You'll then use the lessons and skills you've learned on your next assignment: second in command of a submarine as Executive Officer (XO).

Teacher

During my last year on board HMS *Turbulent*, I was told I'd been selected to teach submarine captains on Perisher. As well as being an absolute honour, I knew it would be a challenge. I also saw what an opportunity it was. The more I thought about it, the more encouraged I was about the idea of what I could achieve. It would be a great way to give back to the rest of the fleet, levering off what my team and I had learnt over the past three years on *Turbulent*, especially during our last, long deployment.

Before I started teaching Perisher in January 2012, as Commander of Sea Training, I led a small team of experts providing training to all attack submarines in the fleet. During this period, the Royal Navy selected me for the Windsor Leadership Programme (the first part of the strategic leadership journey). It was an invaluable experience. The lessons I learned from so many other great leaders from a range of different sectors and industries enhanced and enriched the leadership lessons I'd learned as CO of HMS *Turbulent*. When planning my Perisher course, I drew on these as well as techniques honed by experts in the Royal Marines and Scottish Police I'd learned from the silver commanders' course.

I planned my version of Perisher meticulously. There are some elements that stand the test of time, and there are others that don't. I thought about all of these as I designed the course. I spoke to as many previous teachers as I could including Sir Sandy Woodward, who commanded the Task Force of the Falklands War. It was clear to me what I could change and what didn't need changing. I wanted to introduce 21st Century techniques, particularly focusing on teaching leading out of context. This way, I hoped to expose my trainees to a broader range of leadership skills than those promoted by the submarine service. I put a lot of thought into how I wanted to present my message. Rather than tell my students *how* to lead, instead I wanted them to learn *the moment* to lead.

It was also essential my students understood I was there for their sake and not for my own career progression. Standing there in Nelson's cabin on HMS Victory to welcome them that first day, I told them I was leaving the Royal Navy. My admission set the tone for the course. They understood immediately I was there *only* for them and that this was about their success. Pure and simple. Having established this, I continued:

> "This is your course. You were selected and therefore you must be good enough. I'm here to make you better, but I have a responsibility to the Submarine Service — to make sure you are the best. This is the first stage of your journey and it is a fitting privilege to start here – where Nelson, the father of modern naval leadership, lived and died.

Leadership. We'll discuss this throughout the course; there is no one answer. But it is the cross-exchange of ideas that is vital, the personal approach that becomes strength. Whatever it is, it is great to lead people. Supporting leadership, the best captains, in my view, have faith in what they do, and they choose their companions well. They are good warriors because they understand the space in which they operate. And they understand strategy.

Nelson. There is so much inspiration to be gained from him and I could talk about the Nile, Trafalgar or other battles. But instead of focussing on 1805, I thought I would concentrate on his doubt. In 1777, he wrote in his diary of his feeling that he might never rise in his profession:

'My mind was staggered with a view of the difficulties I had to surmount. I could discover no means of reaching the object of my ambition. After a long gloomy reflection, a sudden glow of patriotism – I will be a hero! And confiding in providence I will brave every danger.'

I need say no more. Just remember that warfare is a personal battle. Rarely will technology be the key to success. So, this sets the tone — this gives you the challenge. There will be hard times ahead, you know it, you expect it, and you need to learn to deal with it because that is what it is to command a submarine. The endeavour will be worth the pain because command is amazing — serve people, lead people and make a difference."

I looked at each of them, one by one, as I concluded.

"Perisher is tough. The weeks are long, it's mentally draining and tests your physical stamina too. It's scary in parts, particularly when things go wrong, but my objective as Teacher was to ensure my students were prepared and capable. My ultimate responsibility, though, was to the crews these leaders would serve. I wanted to know if these students could lead in the most extreme of operations and bring their crews back safely and do it responsibly, without using 'fear' as a form of control."

Captain Fell, who was the Perisher Teacher between the two World Wars, summarised his views on the submarine captain like this:

> The submariner must be a navigator, and electrician, a torpedo man, a gunnery type, and even a bit of a plumber. He must know men and get on with them; he must use initiative and tact and learn how to enjoy hard living. He must accept responsibility young and not misuse it. There is every reason why he should join and delight in joining submarines, but the greatest joy of all is the companionship, unity and feeling that he is one of a team which only he as Commanding Officer can let down. The supreme moment, the moment of truth for the Commanding Officer is in his attack; then, his judgement and actions alone can bring success, failure or death. He has no one to hold his hand, to advise or correct a fatal move. His eye alone can see, and his instincts sense the correct and only tactic to pursue; on him rests all responsibility. When he feels the faith of his Ship's Company behind him, knows that they trust him and will carry out or even anticipate his slightest command, then indeed he is a proud man.

Although submarines are more complex now than they were in Fell's day, in many respects, his words still hold true. The fact that a submarine captain is a warfare officer who is generally not a 'specialist' (for example, a marine engineer is an expert in nuclear power while a weapon engineer is an expert in weapon systems) yet has to make decisions concerning warfare, nuclear engineering, mechanical engineering, weapon engineering, intelligence, rules of engagement, onboard policy, health and safety, equality and diversity, the Armed Forces law, the media, political engagement among others, all while leading people is not insignificant.

During my time as Teacher from 2012 to 2014, I passed most of the student captains. I failed some too. Those I failed fell broadly in two categories: those who seemed unable to control their emotions; and those who lacked the necessary decision-making ability essential to submarine command.

Now it's time to take you on part of that journey. It's a tough one but it will help you demonstrate to the teams you lead that you're worthy of serving them.

On the Bridge

HMS *Triumph* Course 180 Speed 6Kt.
Depth: surfaced. Weapon Readiness state 3.
Area: Clyde Exercise Areas. Transiting. Chartered Depth:
110M. 1130 ZULU.
Captain has conduct. You are the Duty Commanding
Officer.

The bridge of a submarine is an amazing place to be. It's a little like sailing because you can't hear any noise from ventilation or machinery. There's not much in the way of equipment: a pelorus (sighting device); a couple of small bridge windows, there to shield you from the wind but offering little protection; a couple of microphones; a bleep phone; a bridge bag with some tools in it; and a man overboard marker (God forbid you fall in…). And there's really only space for two to move around — the Officer of the Watch (who is in charge) and the Lookout.

In the fin, behind the bridge, is another area called the Radar Mast Well. When this is open to visitors, other crewmembers can go up there to gather and enjoy the fresh air. If the submarine is overt and close enough to land they might even be able to make a phone call too.

Being on the bridge makes you really respect the sea in all its moods. From flat calm, in warm and sunny weather, to the roughest, and sometimes scariest conditions and everything in between. When a submarine is on the surface, it usually means you're going in and out of a harbour or transiting somewhere. Submarines are always going to or coming back from somewhere — on operations that somewhere is generally not a friendly place to be but when you're on the surface on the way back, you know the mission is over and happiness awaits.

You're either coming home or visiting a port (which is known as a 'run ashore') and that means you'll have a chance to recuperate.

It's the start of the sea phase of Perisher and you're on the bridge with the Officer of the Watch and the Lookout. The next four weeks are make or break. You know you'll tested both physically and mentally; you know you'll become exhausted. Teacher told you all in the pre-briefing that the first few days of each phase of Perisher are for training. He'll tell you when it switches to assessment but you already feel like everyone is looking at you. The crew is assessing you all, wondering whether they'd want any of these Perisher students as their captain.

You've been Duty Captain from joining the submarine and will be until the submarine has dived. You really enjoyed manoeuvring the submarine out towards the diving position, doing some Man overboard drills and taking reports as the crew prepared. Teacher stood in the Radar Mast Well talking to the *Triumph's* Executive Officer (XO) for most of this time, while the Attack Coordinator continually monitored and communicated with the Casing Party (the team who manage deck operations) as they stowed their kit under the casing safely after the Boat transfer.

That was only a few hours ago. Now the submarine is at Diving Stations and you take your last breath of fresh air before living off air produced by the submarine.

"Officer of the Watch, Duty Captain going below," you say and start descending the vertical ladders through the conning tower into the Control Room. As your foot touches the deck, the Planesman's voice announces over the microphone. "Duty Captain is below."

Taking off your foul-weather jacket and binoculars, you glance around the control room. All the positions are manned, reports are coming in with various statuses and the Watchleader is coordinating the information. Looking over at Ship Control, you see the XO and the Attack Coordinator discussing the dive. You think about the fact the XO passed Perisher on the last course, and here he is six months on coaching another student. Over at the plot Teacher and the Captain are looking at the WECDIS screen. They don't stay there for long and head off to the Captain's cabin.

The crew is continuing final preparations to dive the submarine. It's a complex procedure but because everyone is trained, processes are happening. The tactical picture is being compiled by the operations team and the periscope and sonar. The navigation team is updating the position in WECDIS. Ship Control is making final checks to the submarine's 'trim' having checked all systems work in every mode — primary, secondary and tertiary). The Watchleader is clearing the bridge of crewmembers and equipment and as the Officer of the Watch comes below, he shuts the conning tower hatch.

Multiple reports are coming in, letting everyone know the status of systems, people's locations and the depth of water.

"Officer of the Watch, are we ready to go?" you ask?

"Sir, the submarine is at Diving Stations, the bridge is clear of all personnel and equipment, the bridge board is clear, all systems are checked correct," he replies.

"Duty Captain. Roger." You walk aft to the Captain's cabin and knock.

"Yes, Duty Captain" he says, pulling back the full-length curtain which is there to give him some occasional privacy. Glancing into the cabin you see Teacher is in there with him. By the looks of it, they're planning, a chart is spread out in front of them.

"Sir, we're ready to dive the submarine."

"You know you don't need to tell me," he says in a low voice so the rest of the Control Room don't hear him. "You're the captain, right?" You nod. "From now on, when you Perisher students are taking your turn as Duty Captain, the team needs to see you *being* the captain. If you keep deferring to Teacher or me, it'll be a struggle for them as well as for you. So just do your stuff. I'll intervene if I need to – does that make sense?"

"Yes, sir."

The Captain turns to Teacher. "Teacher, do you agree?" Teacher nods, and you return to the Control Room.

"Plot, Diving brief." you say and the Navigator follows the format, telling the team where they are, that they're allocated to dive there and what the water depth is.

"AC, ready to go?", you ask the AC who is a fellow Perisher student.

"Yes, sir." .

"AC, dive the submarine."

Diving a submarine is a complex series of processes with a few pinch points you need to be wary of. Teacher had talked to you all about it during the shore training phase when you were in the Ship Control simulators.

When he was at Fleet Operational and Standards Training (FOST) as a Command Rider, Teacher had ridden in submarines the world over. He was also fortunate to have served with the Royal Netherlands and US Navies. During the shore training phase when you were in the Ship Control simulators, he shared the benefit of this experience with you all.

"A lesson about diving a submarine I took away from these experiences, was that there are many ways to dive — not just ours. What's more, ours might not be the most efficient."

"When I was in command," he went on, "We used two different procedures. One of them reduced the time it takes to get underwater by 75 per cent. However, we could only use that procedure because we all understood our platform and each other's capabilities and how to recover if it went wrong. Preparation was key. So we used this simulator to practice before going to sea and that's why we're here now, to practice. The simulator staff are very kindly giving you every moment of spare time they have. Use it wisely."

As the main vents open, while you listen to all the reports coming in you look around the Control Room. The planesman is continually calling out the depth as it gradually changes. It feels like an eternity, but in reality, it's minutes. On the surface the depth gauge reads 9.5 metres. At Periscope depth it reads 17.5 metres.

"Depth now 12 metres. 12.2 metres. 12.4 metres. 13 metres. I have the bubble", the planesman says, meaning he has control.

Reports are now coming in over the main broadcast about the state of all the hatches — all in a sequence from forward to aft. "Forward Escape Tower hatch dry all the way through to After Escape Tower hatch dry."

The submarine heads through 17.5 metres, the periscope lowers, and it goes down to 30 metres before the planes are reversed and it starts ascending again.

"6 up keep 17.5 metres," the AC orders and you hear his order acknowledged.

As the submarine reaches 20 metres, the periscope watchkeeper says "Raise Search." There are two periscopes side by side: a search periscope; and an attack periscope. No one likes the attack periscope — it's unwieldy and in the 21st century, the reasons for using it are fast becoming less relevant. "Breaking, clear, one sweep no contacts close," The periscope watchkeeper reports.

"Carry out Long Post Diving Checks and report to DCHQ (Damage Control Headquarters)," comes over the Main Broadcast. You've been sitting in the Captain's chair, intently monitoring everything that's been going on. Teacher and the Captain are still not in the Control Room, you notice, but you know you need to stop wondering where they are and concentrate.

After about five minutes, Ship Control relays a report from DCHQ that Long Post Diving Checks are complete. The AC gives the order to revert from Diving Stations to the Watch Dived. Now we're where we are meant to be, you think. Back in the environment where we're most comfortable — dived operations. It's home — it really is.

CHAPTER 2

Know Yourself

'Your vision will become clear only when you
can look into your own heart. Who looks outside
dreams; who looks inside awakes.'[5]

Carl Jung.

Perisher doesn't just make you a better commanding officer, it
takes you beyond your limits. This teaches you more about yourself
and for a leader, that's crucial. You must know yourself if you're to
get the best from your people because how you operate influences
how others operate. It sounds obvious, but it's amazing how many
leaders, even if they know the theory, don't act on it. Leading without
self-knowledge can harm your team. This is something I experienced
first-hand and used to inform the way I taught Perisher.

I once had the misfortune to serve under a submarine Captain
who was a 'shouter'. While I'd come across the end product of this
command style (fellow officers who were either damaged by it or
who'd adopted a similar approach) until then, I'd never encountered
this command-style first-hand before or witnessed its impact on a
crew. The two years I served under this man were the worst of my
naval career. In fact, they were so bad, I very nearly gave up and left.

This captain wasn't all bad. He was good at dealing with the
politics involved with readying a submarine for operations and he was
always a complete gentleman with anyone who wasn't a crewmember,

[5] Carl Jung to Fanny Bowditch, 22 October 1916, in Carl Jung, Letters 1906-
1950, Vol 1, Taylor & Francis, 2015.

including staff who came aboard for training. Alone with us, however, he was a different person.

His outbursts of irrational anger became the norm. Now, if these had been consistent, we may have been able to adapt and cope with them over time. But they weren't. It was hard to predict what factors influenced a change in his temper and as his moods were impossible to predict, we were all constantly on edge. Whatever his mood was on waking, it would set the tone for everyone on board.

The captain's cabin is very close to the Control Room and the lighting for both is linked. If he hadn't altered the settings in his cabin, raising the Control Room lighting levels meant you'd also be raising his and if the lights came on while he was asleep we'd be for it. No one dared risk it. As a result, even if it were broad daylight outside when we were at Periscope Depth (PD) nobody changed the lighting in the Control Room.

In a steel tube, isolated from the world outside it's easy to lose perspective and when there's no external support to moderate a leader's behaviour, stress builds and is acutely felt by the team. This captain's inconsistency and toxic leadership style caused immense suffering and made us ineffective. Fearing the consequences, we were constantly second-guessing ourselves and became afraid to make independent decisions. It felt as if the enemy wasn't just without, it was within.

Make a mistake and this captain would publicly berate officers, including me. He'd scream in my face even while I was doing my best to recover the situation and would tell me afterwards, in front of everyone, how I'd cost the submarine the entire mission. I still remember the feelings of hopelessness and humiliation, and the pitying looks from other team members mixed with relief that they weren't the target of his anger on this occasion.

The effect of this on a person internally is devastating. You'll throw up before you go on watch because you can't deal with what's going to happen. This man holds your career in his hands and he's shouting at you, really close to your face and you're looking at your fellow crew members while he's shouting at you. Then factor in that you could be dealing with all this with enemy submarines all around you.

It was during an exceptionally demanding operational patrol that things came to a head. To a man, we'd been apprehensive about this patrol and during the build-up towards it, the Captain's behaviour became more and more erratic. His self-control diminished further and his outbursts increased. He would shout over the most trivial of things. Undoubtedly, this was because of the pressure he was under to achieve but the result was that thousands of miles from any external support, during a patrol against a very capable enemy, the effect of this atmosphere of fear he'd created resulted in things going badly wrong.

These defining moments are where leadership is needed most; you need to step in and take charge. Yet instead of taking direct control of the submarine, the Captain let the team struggle without any direction while he continued to lambast us, keeping up a constant stream of criticism. We were so busy trying to keep thinking ahead of him to avoid any further criticism or anger, we were no longer in a position to outthink the enemy and try and regain control of the tactical situation.

That patrol didn't end well. To make matters worse, it wasn't a one-off, either. Morale on board reduced further and further as this cycle of events continued, throughout the patrol and until the submarine returned to the UK.

Later, after reflection and analysis, I realised most of this captain's issues were created by his being unable to control his emotion. His outbursts were during periods when he may well have been experiencing fear himself: fear of the response of enemy forces and fear of the reaction of his superiors. If a plan wasn't working, instead of interacting directly with the team, he would continue to push us for a solution and criticise us if we did not. You could see this as a way of pushing a team to find its own limits. However, now that I've commanded a crew under exactly the same demanding missions, I don't believe this was the case. Because he wasn't attentive to his own emotional responses and failed to anticipate them, he was unable to control them. If he had, he may have been able to temper his own actions and reduce the impact on the team. Instead, having failed to control his own fear, he transposed it onto others. What's more, I am convinced he was unaware he was doing this.

At a barbecue during a port visit in Gibraltar, I heard this same submarine captain reminiscing with a colleague about a 'shouter' they'd both crewed for some years earlier. He was saying how awful it had been and how this captain's behaviour had created a climate of fear which had been so damaging for the crew. Yet he'd consistently replicated this behaviour. Listening to him talking, it dawned on me that he had no idea he'd adopted this command style. Why? Because he lacked self-knowledge.

Unintentionally, this captain provided me with the greatest preparation for command anyone could have. While I wouldn't understand the burden he was under until I was in command myself, I did now understand the impact of pressure and how knowing yourself, anticipating your emotional responses and being able to control them is essential if you are to serve your team effectively and enable them to achieve success.

Know your limits

During the sea phase of Perisher, the pressure is relentless and it's constantly ramped up. That's deliberate. Teacher is watching you to see how you cope, to enable you to learn your limits. He'll test these and then push beyond them. Why? Because the enemy knows everything about your submarine, its weapons and its capabilities. What the enemy *doesn't* know, are your limits.

While you're busy showing Teacher what you're made of, he's also watching the team supporting you. Will they follow you or not? How you treat people is under observation too. Perisher takes place in front of the junior rates and you need them to help you pass. Negative behaviour, however slight, won't achieve that.

Teacher spends time training you in stress management but until you're at sea on the course, you won't know really how you're going to react. When you're under that much pressure and your career is at stake people can have adverse reactions. And in that steel tube, there's nowhere to hide. It becomes completely apparent what kind of character you are and whether you should have the privilege of leading 130 people on potentially perilous missions autonomously, with nobody there to check your behaviour. Perisher makes you honest with yourself.

Knowing your personal limitations is the first phase of knowing yourself. Do you tire quickly? Then you must manage your sleep. Do you need lots of information to make decisions? Then you must factor in sufficient time to your decision-making process. Do you need physical activity to keep your mind alert? Make time for it.

But before you start on your journey to self-awareness, ask yourself the most important question: why do you want to lead? Are you doing this for yourself or others?

In this second half of the chapter we'll explore:

1. How to better understand yourself
2. The importance of knowing why you want to lead
3. What integrity is and why it matters
4. The value of physical and mental fitness
5. Recognising your triggers
6. Knowing when to step aside.

How to better understand yourself

There are countless articles about authenticity (the quality of being genuine and true); in some organisations, it's regarded as a prime leadership value. Authenticity has been described as 'being yourself' but the fact is few of us have been allowed to 'be ourselves'. At home, you'll conform to your family dynamics; at school, you'll conform to school rules (or not and face some form of discipline).

Then when you leave school and start working, you'll conform again. So 'being yourself' is not always possible.

What you *can* do is understand yourself. The better you're able to understand who you are, what you can't change and what you can, the easier it is to actively influence your own leadership journey.

We all have strengths; we all have weaknesses, and they evolve over time. We all have subtle intricacies; some things make us laugh, make us cry, make us scared, make us happy and when we interact with others, we also need to negotiate everyone else's idiosyncrasies. We are all flawed.

As a starting point, you may find it helpful to use a platform to analyse your personality. There are many platforms you can use for this — Myers-Briggs, OCEAN and MMPI to name a few. I've undergone this profiling in each of my roles since being selected for command and while comparing the results over the years shows an adaptation in some of the measured elements, there's been no real change in my personality. This is to be expected. If you haven't already undergone psychometric analysis, I'd encourage you to take time out and invest in doing one of these tests. If only because it gives you real data that are compared to millions of others around the world.

An assessment in a comparable format of who you are at a particular moment of your journey will give you a lot of information. So what do you do with that information? Having looked through it, do you just file it away? Or do you review it at regular intervals? The answer will vary from individual to individual and depends on your personal needs. However, I would encourage you to fix a time to regularly review the report. And make it a priority, otherwise, you will drift in your leadership journey.

Know why you want to lead

Ask yourself the 'why?' question. Why do you want to lead? Is this something you've wanted to do since you were a child? Is it a passion? Is it a step to something else? Is it for the experience (good or bad)?

Is it being forced upon you and you are a reluctant leader? These questions are really important to understand at many points during the leadership journey.

Understanding 'the why' will help you determine the 'what' and potentially the 'how'.You need to know from the outset that the leadership journey has both ups and downs, successes and failures. It's not for everyone, but if you choose it and make a difference, then the reward is significant (and I'm not talking about the financial reward here but the reward that comes from knowing you made an impact).

Fast forward to the business world and having worked in both FTSE 100 companies and Small and Medium Enterprises (SMEs) I always asked the same question of everyone I spoke to: Why do you want to lead? I'd then follow this up with a series of questions to ascertain the reality. More importantly, I've always asked myself the same question. 'Why do I want to lead?'

Most would come up with a stock answer: they wanted to be the CEO or reach a board position in a particular field. When you delved deeper, however, the majority were saying this because they felt they had to say it. It was what they thought needed to be heard — they didn't want to appear without ambition.

As a mentor, I aimed to get people comfortable with enjoying the leadership journey at every stage until they worked out what they really wanted to do within an organisation, determining where they fit into the team as either leader or follower.

What questions should you consider when working out the 'why'? There is only one. Why do you want to lead? At the outset, there are no right or wrong answers, it's only later in the leadership journey your answer will change.

When interviewing potential mentees I would start by asking them the question. Here are some of the reasons they gave:

- Don't know really
- I want to be the CEO
- I want to advance my career

- I want to make a difference
- I want to be remembered for being a good leader
- I want to serve others
- All my contemporaries are – I should too
- It's good money
- I'd rather not be told what to do
- It's the only way I can get things done
- I have to because of my skills
- I don't want to, but I'm being put in that position.

None of those answers is wrong. Nor are they right. The process always starts for a combination of reasons and as long as you know the answer to the question initially but accept it will evolve over time, then you're on the first step of the journey.

Now that I am self-aware, I realise I never knew from the start how I wanted to lead or who; I did want to do something special. I know that as I progressed within the Royal Navy, my personal narrative (the narrative I formed and told myself) was that I'd always wanted to lead, to be the captain of a submarine. Deep reflection and analysis of 26 years of meticulously written reports by those who led me in the Royal Navy tell a different story.

During my early career, I was uncertain about what it was I wanted to do. I was 'flighty' but evidently, I was capable of getting people to do what they needed to do and make it because they wanted to. I know I was flighty because I would look at others above me in rank and think, I can do your job and better than you are doing it – why do I have to wait to progress?

All my superiors' reports have some commonality: I could communicate well and people would follow; I was 'of average intelligence'; I was passionate; and I was fit. But what's most interesting is how my leadership evolves as I get closer to the privilege of submarine command. The marked change occurs after I completed 'Perisher'. Then everything was about preparation for potential command – I wanted to get it right for my team because I'd seen how brilliant command could be but how poor it could be too.

For some, learning about yourself is an instinctive process. Most of us, however, need to develop a sense of discipline. This is amplified in the early stages of the leadership journey. Behaviours manifested in the early stages, become amplified unless you put in a process to be able to manage them. The further you get into the journey, the harder it becomes. You keep doing what you've always done or you adapt, there's very little in between. The earlier you can get this right, and establish an evolving process over time, the more effective your leadership journey is.

One brilliant option is finding someone who can be objective with you and act in your best interests by providing objective, critical feedback. Proper feedback is really important. The next challenge is learning to be reflective and acting on the feedback.

What is integrity and why does it matter?

Personal standards are really important and don't just develop overnight. How you carry yourself professionally, translates across into your personal life too. The starting point is developing integrity. The word comes from the Latin *integritatem* meaning 'soundness, wholeness, completeness', which in the mid-fifteenth century became 'soundness of moral principle and character'. In the 21st Century, integrity has come to mean what you do when no one's looking. The reason professional integrity is so important is that it underpins much of the activity a leader has to undertake.

Few leaders show absolute integrity all of the time in all areas of their lives. But in my personal view, how you interact with your team requires integrity. This is important, because while we will all make mistakes on occasion, we need to know that we've made a mistake and feel some guilt about it.

When I was in command, I was clear with my team that I wouldn't comment on what they did in their personal lives, whether they gambled, drank, or were unfaithful to their partners — none of it mattered to me as long as it wasn't illegal. I wouldn't encourage it, but their personal life was their personal life. However, if they were unfaithful to our team or behaved in a way that negatively impacted our team, I would have a major issue with it.

No submarine leader gets to choose the crew he or she sails with. You all get put into the steel tube and have to develop as a team. That takes time and means you have to build trust in every person on board, despite their rank or position. Those you feel you can't trust, generally can't be trusted by others. The reason for that? Integrity.

For example, the person who, when asked to do something they don't know how to do, or can't do, doesn't say so. The person who does something for the wrong reason. Those people don't end up staying on board a submarine or in the submarine service. The other members of the team don't trust them, and that person probably doesn't want to be there either.

As a leader, you need to work out what integrity means to you. We're all flawed, after all, and imperfection means that despite our best efforts there will be failures in integrity. Knowing how you are flawed is important. As a leader, you need to determine how you will deal with that.

To create the integrity you want in your team, you need to be able to communicate what that is. In order to communicate what it is, you need to really think about what it means to you.

For submarine captains, I thought it was a simple baseline:

We all have a choice as to how we live and what we do. We all have knowledge and experience so let's make sure we use those for the best. Do not judge people's personal decisions. I will accept that, within our team, people will make mistakes, however, I won't accept wilful negligence. Nor should you.

The value of physical and mental fitness

The physical

In the military, leaders are generally physically fit; they need to be because the job requires stamina. They also need to lead by example. Now, this doesn't mean being faster in a fitness test than a fit 20-year-old, but it does mean exceeding expectations for their age.

The benefits of being physically fit are well known, but in a submarine where there is limited space and very little spare time, it's easy to let it go. Most of the roles onboard test your mind but they are pretty sedentary. You sit in the same position watching a screen and the furthest you can walk in one go is less than 20 metres.

You're tired at the end of each six-hour watch and you know you've got to eat, relax, sleep, wake up, eat and go on watch in the 6 hours you have off. You have to find time to exercise and there are no running machines onboard the attack submarines.

There will be leaders who say exercise isn't necessary, but I think it is. For two reasons: fitness and example.

Being fit gives you physical resilience, which is vital during stressful situations, and all leaders experience stressful situations. When you're stressed (and again, all leaders experience stress), there are a variety of physical effects as your body prepares for a 'fight or flight' response to that particular situation. The release of hormones triggers automatic responses, such as an increase in heart rate and faster breathing to prepare for whatever the response is. Managing the physical elements of stress needs a degree of fitness. Long-term leadership challenges require the same – it really is difficult to effectively manage long-term issues without being fit and creating time to maintain your fitness level.

Leading by example is a vital element of leadership we'll discuss in more detail later on. The benefits of being fit for a leader (to maintain physical resilience and cope with the physical symptoms of stress) are just as applicable to your team members. You demonstrate the example and the benefits.

Perisher tests fitness in a different way, particularly at sea. Sleep is in short supply, you have to make decisions while you are sleep-deprived and you have to learn when not to make decisions. Only if you understand your physical self, can you tell when you are reaching that tipping point — the point at which you are no longer capable of making a rational decision and need rest.

The mental

Mental health is rightly recognised seriously now; that has not always been the case. There is much written about how to look after your own mental health, in fact, almost too much. Most of them involve some form of dialogue with someone – it's OK to ask for help when you're not alright. However, while I was in command, I wouldn't. You're the leader, right? You need to be strong all of the time – the team need a leader who is steadfast. I described it as developing resilience – learning to be resilient naturally, and having mechanisms to cope with trauma as well as those tough moments. For me, this was about reading books and playing my guitar.

I didn't realise my reading was a coping mechanism until it was pointed out to me by a leader outside of the military. They were right. The books I read were either leaders' biographies and autobiographies or analyses of military leadership. What I was doing was using those to help me justify my own decision-making and thus reduce stress.

It was also important for me to do something totally non-military, so I would play the guitar. I can't read music, but I can use tablature and playing took my mind off everything else. It was time spent on me, and that really helped my mental health. I would encourage Perisher students to find that thing — be it reading, playing a musical instrument, drawing, or painting — some hobby that takes them away from the now, allows them to relax, and helps protect their mental health.

In the business world, the amount of information you have to absorb and the constant demands of continuous communication can have a serious impact on your stress levels — particularly if you're not trained to deal with stress.

The translation from Perisher is that all leaders should find something that can give them perspective for the challenge at hand.

For me, it was concentrating on the last worst thing that happened to me and then finding some solace that whatever challenge I was currently facing wasn't as bad as that – unless it was.

My tragic experiences began as a child before my 6th birthday. I had an awful four years and then things changed considerably. That became my anchor – if things went wrong, I would say to myself, "It's not going to be as bad as that" and inevitably it wasn't. Even after my mother's suicide, I deployed the same coping tactic. In retrospect, how awful is that? I told myself that my mother's death wasn't as bad as a series of horrendous things that happened to me as a young adult.

Then one day in 2011, when it really was nearly over onboard HMS *Turbulent*, that tactic stopped working. Why? Because now it wasn't about my individual experience and the effect on me personally, it was about everyone else, those people I was responsible for. What was each of them thinking about their own survival — about which they could do nothing on a personal level? The strange thing about being onboard a submarine is that you cannot do anything personally to control your own survival. You all survive or you don't. I concentrated on trying to recover the situation. In hindsight, you'd expect nothing less from a leader, and I'm convinced my personal resilience has been created through the combination of having to deal with some significant situations throughout my life and through training.

Not everyone can train themselves to deal with issues and manage their mental health, but we all need to find a method that works for us personally. We're all different, therefore no one solution type will work. You may find mental health training increases your resilience. Or you may find it doesn't. For many people, meditation is an effective stress reducer and a way of creating a space for inner stillness. For others, training for a marathon or hiking can help ground you and make you feel work pressures are more surmountable (it'll help with your physical fitness levels too). If music isn't your thing, find something else you enjoy. There's really no one-size-fits-all approach. Try different things, experiment, and find out what works for you.

Recognising your triggers

We are human and we all have triggers. It could be a colleague arriving late to a meeting for the umpteenth time, or a business partner criticising an idea. Whatever your trigger is, your amygdala (the part of your brain associated with emotional processes) becomes overwhelmed or 'hijacked' and before you know it, you're lashing out in anger or just shutting down.

As a leader, identifying your triggers will give you valuable insight and information about what is a problem for you and how to manage your reactions. Because you do have agency over how you respond to a trigger. It's vital you learn how to manage them before they get the better of you and provoke an unwarranted response.

Most people have several triggers. Rather than trying to identify all of them at once, you may find it easier to focus on the three you find most affect your work life.

So, how do you go about this?

1. Dig down into what happened

First, you need to understand what comes before your reaction. Ask yourself questions to dig down into what's happened. For example:

- Was it something someone said? Was it *how* they said it? Or was it the words used? Does the context make a difference?
- Or is it an action? If so, is it a one-off that triggers you or does it take repeated occurrences before you explode?
- Are you anxious about things going on in your life outside of work or is everything in your personal life going swimmingly?

2. How are you interpreting what happened?

Next, work out what you're telling yourself when this happens. Triggering isn't about what someone is saying or doing, it's about the story you're telling yourself. When someone criticises your work are you upset because you think you're incapable?

Everything people say or do is about them, not you. But what you hear and see is about you. Work out what meaning you're ascribing to what's been said or done. Are you interpreting it in a way that's triggering you?

3. Spot the physical signs

We all have 'tells' — physical symptoms that we're about to erupt in anger or shut ourselves down. What are yours? Does your face flush? Does your heart rate noticeably quicken? Does your stomach turn over?

These physical signs may manifest themselves before you even realise you're upset. Learn to spot them by noting your physical reactions.

4. Pushing the 'stop' button

Having identified your triggers, you can then start working out how to manage your instinctive reaction and push the 'stop' button. Everyone's different, what works for you may not work for other people. But there are several things you could try:

- When you notice those telltale physical symptoms, stop thinking. Instead, focus on your breathing. You might need two or three inhale/exhales, or you might need ten or twenty. It doesn't matter. Find out what's best for you.
- Change your circumstances, immediately. The great thing about the business world is that nothing is immediately catastrophic - you at least have minutes. You might find you only need to open a window. Alternatively, you might need to leave the building and go for a walk. The important thing here is to do whatever you feel you need to do to avoid losing your temper.

- Practice stopping your thoughts. As humans, we're blessed with an imagination that can sometimes get the better of us. Learn to curb this and reinterpret the story you're telling yourself by deliberately stopping your thoughts before they cause you a problem.

Know when to step aside

Before I took up my post as Perisher Teacher I did the Scottish Police's Silver Commanders' Course. I did this so I could expose my students to a wider range of techniques than the submarine service offers. I had to do it first before they did. In retrospect, I realise the Scottish Police wanted to see how far I could be pushed before I cracked so they threw some really hostile simulated activity into the mix.

On one occasion I was coordinating the team as we navigated a massive gas explosion and high-speed police chase all at the same time. I'd suggest something and a member of the Fire Service would say, "We're not doing that." So I'd come up with something else, to which a member of the Ambulance Service would reply, "That's a really stupid idea."

Eventually, I pulled both men together.

"Look," I said. "All I want is the right outcome so if I'm not the person to lead this, I will gladly step into a support role and one of you can take over. You just decide who it is and I'll gladly step aside".

At that, they turned around and said "No. You're the one who's leading it." And from that moment on, everything came together.

Knowing when to take the lead and when to step aside is the hallmark of good leadership. By stepping back and letting others take a turn at the wheel you're serving your team, allowing other leaders to develop.

Pressure points:

- Know why you want to lead
- Learn to be reflective and take feedback
- Recognise your triggers
- Know when to lead and when to step aside.

Eyes only

HMS *Triumph*. Course 180. Speed 3K.
Depth: 17M (periscope depth).
Patrol Quiet state. Weapon Readiness state 3.
Area: Clyde Exercise Areas. Chartered Depth: 120M. 0810 ZULU.
Captain has conduct. You are the Duty Commanding
Officer.

It's the start of the Periscope safety phase or 'Eyes only'. You did well in this during the shore phase, so you're feeling confident. Teacher told you all it would be harder at sea — it's a less responsive platform than the simulator because it's real! Real sea conditions, real frigates, real risk and, most importantly, real people putting their lives in your hands.

You look at your fellow students dotted around the control room. The US student looks nervous. The relationship between the US and UK submarine forces is very tight. It goes back a long way. It's not the first time a US student has attended this coveted course, and it won't be the last. They generally send their best and it's impressive how well he's adapted to new processes, procedures, tactics and, importantly, a different culture.

There's also been another complication with the course. All the Perisher students had to spend time on both a Dutch and Norwegian submarine to learn their approaches to managing safety at periscope depth. You could take it or leave it after finishing the course, Teacher said, but it was a unique experience. You enjoyed that couple of days.

The 'eyes only' process tests your spatial awareness and mental maths, how well you calculate under pressure and involves some decision-making. But it's not an intellectual process nor does it pitch you against the next man to see who wins.

However, it does give you a real sense of confidence when operating close to warships. Which comes in handy, as every captain knows!

The aim is to remain at periscope depth in the presence of close-proximity warships. You need to know where the warships are, determine where they are going to be, and work out whether you can stay at periscope depth or must go deep. To calculate this, there's a set process to follow:

- First locate the ship and the bearing (noting the position relative to yours).
- Then 'split the image'. This gives you a measurement of minutes.
- Divide into the height of the ship (+15 %).
- X 1000 = gives you the range
- Assume (until proven otherwise) that the ship is travelling between 26-29 knots.
- Know that your speed to go deep is 7kts therefore closing speed is 36 knots.
- At 36 knots the distance closed is 1200 yards in 1 minute, which = 100 yards in 5 seconds.
- It takes you 1 minute to go deep to a safe depth under the ship. So if it reaches 1200 yards you must go deep.

Here's an example:

Split the image (14 minutes), divided into a height of 40 = 2.8 x 1000 = 2800 yards.
2800 -1200 yards = 1600
1600/1200 = 1 with 4 left over. 4 x 5 secs=20 secs. 1 min 20 secs.

Now do that for 4 ships, all going at different speeds and within different ranges, as well as leading your team and controlling the submarine!

Teacher told you no natural ability was required for this, but he also said others disagreed. Anyway, that's all behind you. Now to the task at hand.

"Team, we're going to start with two ships," Teacher says. "This is training. I don't mind if you make mistakes as long as you learn from them quickly. So if I take you deep in the first few days, don't worry, just learn from it. I'll tell you when you're being assessed. Today each one of you will do around four visual safety runs. Make the most of the recovery time, so we can increase intensity rapidly." He looks directly at you. "You're up first."

Picking up the Main Broadcast microphone he then makes an announcement to the Ship's Company. Thanking them in advance, he tells them it's going to be different to the patrol they've just finished, how they're making a difference and it begins here. You look around at the crew. They're engaged. You see Teacher glance at *Triumph*'s Captain and nod.

You approach the Attack periscope. It's called the Attack Periscope because the top of it is tiny, it's designed to allow you to get really close to ships and land without anyone seeing it. [6]

After checking the multitude of stopwatches laced into your belt and hanging around your neck to see they're running, you look back at Teacher. "Ready, Sir."

'Start the run," Teacher says. It begins.

---

[6] In the 21st Century, this is less relevant because you need the sensors on the Search Periscope to achieve 'effect'. In the military 'effect' is used to mean having the desired effect on your enemy or potential enemy: to deter, disrupt, suppress or destroy.

CHAPTER 3

Know Your Team

'A leader is best when people barely know he exists, when his work
is done, his aim fulfilled, they will say: we did it ourselves'.

Lao Tzu, *Tao Te Ching*.

It doesn't matter if you're commanding a submarine, running
a small business or CEO of a multimillion-pound organisation, as
a leader you need to figure out how to work with people in a close,
often intense environment and help them grow. To do this effectively,
you need to know the people and personalities you're leading — your
team. The larger the team, the more difficult this becomes but you
should be able to manage it up to about 130 people.

A change in one of your team's performance affects everyone and
without understanding each person well, you won't know how best
to help them. And it's not just your team you need to know either.
You should make a conscious effort to know everything about their
families too.

During my time with the Submarine Service, there were two
captains who stood out. You've already heard about one in the
previous chapter and from him, I learned how not to lead. But there
was another who was *the* role model for me, from whom I learned
so much and whose leadership style I chose to emulate: John
Richardson.

I met John when I was seconded to the US Navy in 2005 having
been selected as the UK submarine exchange officer with Submarine
Development Squadron 12. It was a great opportunity to learn from
a different group of submariners and in return, provide them with

a different perspective. However, working with John was the biggest benefit of the entire experience.

A truly selfless leader, John was about everyone else and never himself; nothing he did was ever to further his own ambitions. Whether you were a junior submariner or an admiral, he paid you the same attention. He would fight those fights he needed to, but back off and empower others when appropriate. He never appeared flustered. In all the time I worked with him, I only once saw him show signs of stress during a live torpedo firing — and even then it was imperceptible to everyone else.

What I really admired about John was the way he encouraged the crew's families to be part of the team and made a point of looking after them. Submariners' families play a crucial role, yet this is not often acknowledged. When your partner, sibling, parent or child is away at sea for long periods, often uncontactable for weeks, it can put a huge strain on relationships. It's stressful for everyone. John understood that, in his role as a leader, easing this strain as much as possible was imperative. While I was working with John I decided that when my time came I, too, would include crewmembers' families in the team.

Know and be known

In advance of Perisher, I supplied all student captains with a collection of advice gleaned from my experience as a submariner and captain: *A Guide to Taking Command*. It's still used today. Here's an extract from Chapter Four: Your Team:

'The people who live together in the close company of a submarine need a corporate source of inspiration, a directive symbol to look to. The abstract idea of the Submarine or Service doesn't meet this instinctive need. This feeling of trust and dedication must be in a person. Naturally, that person should be the CO.

The art of command is to be the complete master and yet shipmate of every person on board; the temporal lord but the spiritual brother of every rating; to be detached and yet not remote. The basis of this art is to know your people and be known by them. For some, this will be easy, for others it will take considerable work to achieve – but you must achieve it to be successful.'

On Perisher, knowing your team and being known by them is difficult on the shore phase as teams vary from week to week. But during your concluding weeks at sea, you only have two teams to consider — each watch. Submarines work in a two-watch system. Two separate teams take turns: six hours on, six hours off. Each team also operates differently – personality affects a lot. Moreover, the interactions between the individuals within the team are different. It takes a real leader to understand all of those. In this respect, Perisher is a baptism by fire — and a quick-fire one at that. But it's a key lesson for would-be captains. Teacher will be watching how quickly you get to know a new team and how well you adapt to changes in personnel for good reason.

I said earlier, you don't get to choose your crew, and that's a good thing — you have to form your crew, mould one you inherit until it's almost perfect, noting it will never be perfect. You may be able to influence a few selections, but otherwise, you pretty much have to accept the hand you're dealt, which is typically a cross-section of modern society in a 'tin can'. You won't all have similar backgrounds, nor will you share the same interests and along with those you consider normal in approach, there will be some who break rules, some who are violent and some with problems. Differences in education levels will be extremely marked too, ranging from a Master's degree in nuclear physics to a single GCSE. But because the missions submarines undertake are so sensitive, risky and important — militarily, strategically and politically — both parties must make it work.

The crew is already onboard when you arrive at the submarine for Perisher's sea phase and is established, having been there for several weeks already. So, while you only have two teams to consider, you're faced with getting to know a new crew fast, in the same way you would as a captain. In the business world, this happens too. Unless you're running a start-up, or you've been brought into a company to create a team from scratch, you'll usually be taking over from someone else.

Passing Perisher doesn't mean you're automatically respected and can take over command anywhere. My first command after 20 years in the Royal Navy was the attack submarine HMS *Turbulent*. I was 38. I joined the crew in 2009, one-third of the way through operational sea training. I would be taking over a tough, well-established team who, while undoubtedly tired, had still to complete training and were already behind schedule. I knew I had to get to know my team and they had to get to know me. Fast. They didn't need to like me but it was essential for me to be respected and have their trust and loyalty.

Assuming command for the first time is one of the greatest steps you will ever take. It embraces not only the responsibility for one of His Majesty's Submarines but the power to influence an entire team; the power to enable as opposed to constraining, and the ability to make a measurable difference. The Submarine Service is different in that, while it carries the historic tradition of dignity, there is little 'privilege'. The real return is the sense of achievement, the knowledge that your leadership enabled your team and your submarine to achieve success.

I wanted to ensure the crew of *Turbulent* was the best team. Not the best we could be, *the* best. But before I could motivate the crew to work with energy and enthusiasm towards our shared goal and ensure they were armed with the skills and tools they needed to do this, I had to find out who I was dealing with. I decided not to take the traditional approach.

Most captains line up the entire ship's company on the jetty and give a long speech. In my experience, this often ends up being a long-winded monologue about themselves. I decided to do things differently. Instead of assembling the whole crew and giving the traditional, long, inaugural address, I chose to talk to a handful of people at a time and speak for no more than a minute and a half. I rehearsed this in advance, careful to minimise distracting hand movements or mannerisms. My children were my audience and critics: did I come across as arrogant or confident? Did I sound like I was talking down?

When the time came, I walked into the room, introduced myself to the handful of people standing there and said:

"Hi, I'm Ryan and this is what I look and sound like. We've got a hard journey ahead. We will have some challenges, but we will be successful. In the coming weeks, I will take time to get to know you, and you will get to know me. In the meantime, I need your honesty and commitment."

I only varied this short speech when giving it to senior crewmembers. I wanted to talk specifically about leadership with them as they were also in leadership positions. To the officers, therefore, I added several sentences:

'We need to lead by example, step up to the mark, and make our teams do great things. We are leaders because we are skilled and motivated. I look forward to working with you."

I also gave each member of the leadership team a letter including a one-page outline of our ethos as a baseline which, I explained, could be adapted.

After those first introductory talks, I made a conscious effort to create the time to get to know my crew and understand each and every one of them.

Walk the teak

On HMS *Turbulent* the crew numbered 160 personnel in all, although you usually sail with around 130. Because you're away for long stretches, you need to rotate people. Some may have to return to land for training courses to further their career, or to take leave. You may sometimes need specialist riders for certain types of operations and be required to carry trainees from other submarines too.

It's surprising how different a team can look after only a few crew changes. As a leader, your challenge is managing the personalities of both new and existing hands, ensuring the whole team integrates and quickly settles down. The most effective way of doing this is to get around the crew, see everyone and find out how they are.

On Perisher, captain's rounds are a good opportunity to interact with crew in different departments and get to know them. In naval terms, this is known as 'walking the teak', a relic of HMS Victory days when teak was used for deck-planking and officers paced the quarter-deck checking on the boat and its crew.

Getting to know your team is more difficult in the business world. On a submarine you don't go home every night – you live together, breathe together, eat together, win together, lose together, survive together or die together. With the exception of his own cabin, a captain has no privileges above those enjoyed by the crew. He shares the same food, the same atmosphere, the same toilet and, most importantly, he has made the same journey to become a qualified submariner. The combination of all of these elements means a submarine commander can easily understand the challenges faced by the team at every level.

Employees nowadays have a choice where they work. They do their research and pick a company that's well-led (or so they hope). Chances are, they won't have had the same journey as you or faced the same obstacles to get there. It's down to you to find the common ground.

Everyone has different motivations for being in a team — service, money, survival, or a career move — and it's not always easy to work this out. In every organisation I've worked I've spent considerable time listening to people and trying to ask the right questions. I need to know my team, the personal dynamics, listen to what they have to say and not judge because they don't have the same motivations as me. It's important because if suddenly someone is not performing as they have been, you can ask questions based on a personal relationship to find out if you can help.

When I joined National Grid as Head of Construction in March 2016, my portfolio was countrywide. Now, I could have stayed put in the company headquarters in Warwick, never leaving the building. Instead, I decided to 'walk the teak' by travelling the length and breadth of the country to meet the team. It meant a lot of driving, but it was invaluable. As far as I'm concerned, face-to-face time is the *only* way to properly get to know your people. You're able to read far more from body language and micro-expressions face-to-face than you can by looking at someone on a screen.

Share a little — it goes a long way

A difficult childhood and the submarine service taught me resilience, and enabled me to hide emotions and learn to cope. But unless your team members are completely resilient, personal issues will always impact their performance. As a leader, you need to ask questions and build trust. Share a little about yourself, and show some vulnerability (but not too much) to enable people to engage.

I'll give you an example. On a mission to the Mediterranean, we surfaced the submarine as we passed through the Straits of Gibraltar or STROG as we call it. The gateway between the Atlantic and Mediterranean, it's an amazing place. I went up onto the bridge for this part of the transit and five members of my crew joined me. Everyone welcomes the chance to come up to the bridge. You can enjoy a bit of fresh air, take in the scenery slipping past, call home if there's a signal, and enjoy a smoke before we dive again. You might even catch sight of a dolphin swimming alongside. It's also a great opportunity for an informal chat.

On this occasion, someone probably said something like "I wonder what Gibraltar's like as a run ashore". Inevitably, someone on the bridge will have an amusing anecdote to share and this time it seemed appropriate to recount my first time there.

"The first time I went to Gibraltar was as a midshipman on the HMS *Sheffield* in 1990. I partied hard, but I was also the sports officer on board, so I was responsible for organising the traditional Rock Race. As you all know, Gibraltar Rock is over 350 metres high and hard work to run up even if you're fit and sober. Doing it hung over wasn't pleasant. I vividly remember the captain showing real disappointment that his sports officer ended up so far back in the field."

Out of the corner of my eye, I saw grins exchanged and heads nod at my candidness. "I walked back down with a fellow midshipman," I continued, "As we arrived at the place where most of the apes loiter, for some reason, he decided to push one of them. I couldn't believe it! At first, the ape looked disgusted, then angry and then clearly communicated with the other apes. I knew then this would end badly but wasn't going to hang around to see what they did next. I started running and shouted to my mate to run too. Hangover or no hangover, I managed to move pretty fast, with the apes close behind. Luckily, the apes gave up eventually. But we didn't stop running till we reached the bottom."

The men laughed, squinting up at the rock and made various quips about the apes looking out for me for revenge. In addition, it removed some of the 'mystique' of being a captain.

When you've established a connection and built trust, if you ask questions, you'll get answers. However, it takes enormous leadership commitment to do that and before you embark on it you need to understand how to engage. Get it wrong and you'll lose people's trust — and that's hard to regain.

How to get to know your team

Whatever the situation, always remember the effect your attitude towards your team will have. Fail to look up and acknowledge a member of staff who's just walked into the room, or take a call during a meeting (even if it's a remote one) and you're setting yourself up for fall. That's exactly the kind of rude behaviour that very effectively tells your people how little you value or respect them. It's the fastest way to alienate them. Instead, demonstrate you rate them highly and you're interested in getting to know them.

The second part of the team equation is learning about each individual team member. Here's how:

- **Make individual time** — don't just use the time to discuss a team member's role, responsibilities and goals. Take the trouble to ask questions about their interests, hobbies, background and families. It'll help you build rapport and establish a connection.
- **Ask the questions that count** — try asking open-ended questions that can't be answered with a simple 'yes' or 'no'. These start with 'why', 'how', 'what', 'describe', 'tell me about' or 'what do you think about'. They'll encourage people to expand their answers and give a longer response which will give you more information and aid insight into their personalities.

For example, instead of asking "Do you like the new project?" ask "What is your experience of the new project?" Ask follow-up questions to encourage team members to expand further.

- **Listen — what leaders all should do** — pay attention to verbal cues like tone, pace and inflection and nonverbal cues — like facial expressions and body language. Avoid interrupting or making assumptions before a person's finished speaking. Clarifying and summarising what's been said shows you're engaged and keen to understand their perspective. It will help you forge stronger relationships, resolve conflicts and improve your communication skills.
- **Operate an open door policy** — if you have to have a separate office, leave the door open (metaphorically at least) and ensure your team knows this. Some employees are shy about putting in requests to see those at the top of the command chain. Be approachable. Your team needs to know you're concerned for

their well-being, both at work and at home and that you're readily available to them.

- **Leave judgement at the door** — approach the conversation with an open mind. Everyone has different experiences, opinions and ideas. If you find you're starting to judge, pause and reflect before responding. Think about what might be influencing your reaction and focus on finding a constructive way forward. By avoiding judgement you're creating a safe, supportive environment where team members feel comfortable sharing their thoughts and ideas. It'll help build trust and strengthen relationships.

- **Put yourself in their shoes** — On *Turbulent,* I introduced regular activities like cooking steaks in the galley every Saturday night. It was sweaty work — serving my team 130 steaks in a two-hour period — but it gave me a chance to experience what the chefs did and opened up a dialogue between us. Think of ways all those in leadership roles could do this within your organisation.

- **Ask "What can I do better?"** — it can give you a more comprehensive idea of how the team is operating, its strengths and weaknesses and invite criticism of your output - how can I improve? You'll then be able to make more informed decisions that benefit the team as a whole.

You can garner feedback in several ways:

1. Schedule individual meetings with each team member. Asking for feedback in a private and confidential setting can encourage openness and honesty about thoughts and opinions.

2. Conduct surveys to gather feedback anonymously. This approach may make team members feel more comfortable providing feedback, especially if the subject matter is sensitive or they'd like to keep their opinion private.

3. In team meetings ask open-ended questions to gather feedback on overall progress, processes that need improvement and success sorties. Allow discussion so team members can bounce ideas off each other.

I've always been wary of over-briefing. On *Turbulent*, I allowed plenty of interaction and encourage ideas from everyone in the team. After all, some of the best ideas often come from those you least expect.

How to inspire your team

Prior to the professional soldier, it was extremely difficult to motivate a conscript or pressed man. Even in the 21st Century, it can still be challenging, despite the professional nature of today's UK fighting forces. Yet, motivate your team you must. Without it, there is no apparent purpose to any endeavour.

Inspiring your team is about creating an environment where team members feel valued, motivated, and engaged. How do you do this? By leading by example, setting clear goals and expectations, encouraging creativity and collaboration, enabling those below you and providing growth opportunities.

Lead by example

Leading by example is vital. In my *Perisher Guide to Taking Command*, I explain why:

'On assuming command, few officers realise the extent their personalities are mirrored in their submarines. The Ship's Company notes every word you say in the Control Room or on rounds, and the Officers mark every word you say in the Wardroom. A display of unwarranted temper, an unjust or over-hasty reprimand, a sloppy piece of ship handling, or an uncloaked show of anxiety, will be commented on by your officers and ratings. At the same time, the way you confront danger has a ripple effect. Your courage will spread to every corner of the submarine.

Not everything will always go right for you or the boat. When things go wrong it's vital you don't give in to despondency and take responsibility for your own and your team's mistakes. It is an essential part of your job to maintain a good submarine spirit and this, in large measure, will be a reflection of you.'

As a Perisher student, you'll be observed during all your interactions with crew members, from officers to junior submariners. What Teacher is looking for is consistency and control of your emotions, even during acute stress. However, cloaking your feelings doesn't mean being cold towards your team. You'll be marked down for this too.

In the corporate world, the same is true. Substitute an enemy submarine for a competitor winning the lucrative new business pitch your team's worked long and hard on and the same gloom will be felt in the office. Your reaction is key.

Hide your disappointment. Take responsibility yourself for the failure and learn from your mistakes. Why didn't it work? What can you learn about yourself and how can you do better in future?

Had you motivated the team properly to begin with? Was the goal crystal clear? Was everyone working together to achieve that same goal? Did they have the training and resources needed to achieve success? Is a member of the team underperforming and that's impacted everyone? If that's the case, you weren't paying attention. If you had been and knew the member of personnel well, you'd have observed a change in them and made it your mission to find out how you could help.

Be honest, remain cheerful and, when necessary, robust. Remember, success is your team's; failure is yours. Having heard too many mission debriefs where captains talk as if success was down to them. Instead of acknowledging the team effort, they'll say 'I detected the frigate and decided to close'. What they should say is "We detected the frigate and decided to close". After all, the captain wasn't sitting on the sonar set reporting to the operations team and identifying the frigate through the periscope. Nor was he putting the navigational fix on to check it was safe, ensuring the power was available. His team did all that. I always use 'we' unless I'm talking about a failure. In which case I use 'I'. On a submarine, we are all in the same boat. Literally and figuratively.

Unleash your team's potential

Believing in yourself can be the best is a self-fulfilling prophecy. When I took command of *Turbulent,* I'd like to think all I did was make the team believe they could do it — and they did.

Ensure you've thought about occasions where you routinely "raise the bar" and demand greater urgency and a higher work rate from the team. During these periods, you may need to spend more time personally directing, but once the team's responded you can let them do the job. They will generally have responded in such a way that the bar, set higher, becomes their new working level.

A wise former Perisher teacher once said: "Prove yourself capable of driving or fighting the submarine once, then let them do it." Command tests both your physical and moral courage but your most important success metric is measured by the generation you empower.

US Lieutenant General Hal Moore explains how to do this succinctly:

'Taking care of your people is not just about the obvious things — pay, working conditions, concern for their welfare and that of their families — but seeing to it they are properly trained...If you discover people who are uniquely talented, give them the tough jobs and mentor them. It's your duty to help them develop their skills and to learn.'[7]

On a submarine, the best training is not given formally, but in the everyday running of it. There are often moments in the Control Room when staff aren't fully occupied. It's a perfect opportunity to carry out or delegate training without team members consciously realising it. Often, an innocently sprung question about, let's say, the action that should be taken in a given emergency will provide food for thought and is highly effective instruction.

There's no reason this can't translate to the corporate world. Look for opportunities to develop individual team members. Encourage their confidence and build their experience so they're ready to take on greater responsibility. As Hal Moore says, "Look for and find the really good 'horses' in your organisation and run them hard. Push them and challenge them with greater levels of responsibility."[8]

If you are to lead effectively, it is imperative that you understand your team properly so you can play to their (and your) strengths and limit the impact of any weaknesses. You should have a clearly communicated idea as to what constitutes 'success' and it needs to be accepted by the team. Inspiration is nothing without vision – your team must know, understand and buy into your vision.

Understand when team dynamics change

Everyone knows a cohesive and productive team is crucial for success in any organisation. However, team dynamics can change — and for a variety of reasons. It could be down to the introduction of new team members or new goals or caused by external factors.

---

[7] Mike Guardia, *Hal Moore on Leadership: Winning when outgunned and outmanned*, Magnum Books, 2017, p.43.
[8] ibid, p.100.

Whatever the cause, understanding when team dynamics change is crucial for adapting and maintaining a high level of performance.

The first sign team dynamics may be altering is a shift in communication patterns. Are team members no longer communicating effectively with each other? Are they avoiding discussions? If so, it could be a red flag. So is a decrease in productivity. If the team is no longer meeting its goals, you may find there are underlying problems you need to address. It's important you identify the cause, whether it's down to a lack of motivation or resources or because the goals are unclear. Only when you've identified the root cause will you be able to take steps to address the issue and get the team back on track.

Whether you're leading a submarine or an organisation, you need a common goal that inspires people to work hard together. What's more, they need to feel they can make a difference. When the scope of your operation changes suddenly (and in the military, this can happen daily) you need the team to be able to adapt and be on board with those changes.

While I was serving as captain of *Turbulent*, I rarely gathered the crew on the jetty. But in 2011 we were ordered to go East of Suez to help with the counter-piracy effort and provide UK Tomahawk (first strike) coverage. Submarines don't hang around off the enemy's coastline waiting for the moment to strike, we need to prepare and plan. That means testing all our equipment and quietness on an instrumented underwater range, practising cruise missile launches, conducting special forces training and planning the journey in advance. All this takes time.

I was pretty confident as I surveyed the crewmen gathered on the jetty before me. By this time, I knew them all well and they knew me. They recognised *Turbulent's* energy and motivation and bought into it. We'd become the team to be a part of and they were proud of that fact.

"You know I don't normally do this," I began, "Well done on where we are today. We've come a long way, but the hardest part of the challenge starts shortly. The commander of operations needs us to deploy as soon as possible. Therefore we need to complete operational sea training (OST) rapidly. I've told him we will be ready in twenty-six days. I've told him that because we *can* be ready in twenty-six days. Because we are motivated. We thrive on success, and we will not fail. I need you to buy into that success, prepare your families for your departure, prepare yourself, and get ready for this difficult journey. That is all".

As I looked around at everyone I saw immediately that two crew members clearly weren't buying into the vision.

Your team's faces offer you the best window into their emotional lives. It doesn't matter what culture you're from, what background you have or what language speak, facial expressions are a universal system of signals we all share and they mirror moment-to-moment changes in our emotional state. There are seven basic emotions universally recognized through facial expressions: happiness, surprise, fear, anger, disgust, sadness and contempt.

As a leader, reading faces is a skill you want to acquire if you don't already have it. You'll be able to recognise when an emotional response is beginning, when an emotion is being concealed, and when a person is unaware of what they're actually feeling.

When someone is trying to conceal what they're feeling, the emotion may often be evident in their face in what's known as a microexpression.[9] An involuntary, subtle muscle movement that lasts half a second or less, microexpressions can't be faked.

We all detect microexpressions on a subconscious level and automatically react to them. But microexpressions are so fleeting, they can be difficult to interpret, but with practice, you can learn to read these on a conscious level as they happen in real-time. It's an invaluable tool to have in your leadership toolkit. It'll not only

---

[9] To keep it simple and show how you can apply this knowledge to business, I'm using the term 'micro expressions' to describe all facial expressions shorter than half a second. However, some of these micro expressions would, scientifically speaking, be more correctly identified as 'partial expressions', 'subtle expressions', or 'masked expressions'.

help you determine if someone's lying or concealing an emotion, it's also a skill you can use to take your team's temperature, gauge their response and identify potential issues quickly before they escalate. But it does require close observation of individuals so you can make a baseline of 'normal' conversational signals for comparison.[10] In this instance, interpreting two crewmembers' microexpressions revealed to me a shift in the team dynamic.

Naysayers, those who criticise or object, can harm team dynamics in any situation but doubly so in the close confines of a submarine. As I addressed the team on the jetty that day and noticed the reactions of those two crewmembers I made a mental note to find out what was required to convince them to buy into the vision. And if they still couldn't, to move them on, responsibly. The mission succeeds only with an engaged team. On *Turbulent,* when I came across problem characters, if I couldn't get them to buy into the vision, rather than pass them on (which just makes them someone else's problem) I removed them from the Navy. It was a year-long process, involving 'quarterlies' — quarterly warnings — which gave them a year to turn themselves around. But it was what was fair for the individual and fair to the Navy.

There's a bell curve in most teams. To the right of the curve, you have those who don't need steering or motivation; they just get on with the job. In the centre of the graph is the majority. They're motivated and want to achieve the end goal but they need direction. To the left of the curve is the third group — the ones who won't budge, whatever the situation. In my experience, leaders spend too much time trying to shift the third group, often at the expense of the other two. Avoid this. Instead, learn to recognise when there's nothing you can do to effect a shift in the stubborn ones' perspectives

---

[10] There are lots of books and courses to help you master this skill. Unmasking the Face, Paul Edkman, Wallace Friesen, Malor Books, 2003 explains how to correctly identify the seven basic emotions and how to tell when people are trying to mask or simulate them. It also has practical exercises to help you hone this skill.

and either isolate or remove them (don't just move them on). And make sure you're fair and compassionate during the process.

I think leaders often shy away from making these difficult decisions. In business, problem characters often just get passed on. I don't believe this is helpful to anyone. So in the corporate world I've adopted the same approach to the one I used when commanding *Turbulent*.

After leaving the Navy, my first job was as Installation Manager for Shell Shearwater, in charge of an oil rig in the North Sea, 225 km east of Aberdeen. My role was to ensure the safety of the 90-odd people who clocked in at the platform. My first day on the job was jaw-dropping. I hadn't reckoned on how big it was; the scale of these things is incredible. I was used to challenges. In the Submarine Service, I'd fought Somali pirates, provided Tomahawk support off Libya, and voyaged under the ice at the North Pole. So when I met the oil rig teams and saw the focus level, I thought 'Bring it on'.

It was still a challenge. I led at $117 a barrel and at $26 a barrel so the difficulty was, how do you maintain productivity, keep up morale and effectively keep everything going during moments of crisis and change? What's more, there were 24 different companies on that oil rig. So I was leading teams with totally different company cultures, trying to get the best out of each individual.

Of course, I 'walked the teak'. I made a point of getting to know each and every one of the 90 people on that rig as individuals. And I observed.

It soon became apparent there were two problems. The first was that productivity was poor. The tool time for people was supposed to be 12 hours a day; we were lucky if we were achieving four. A shift was meant to start at 6 am but the reality was they wouldn't actually do anything until about 7 because they'd have a safety briefing first and then get their work permit which would take until about 8 am. Then it was coffee and bacon roll time which would last until about 9.30 am followed by lunch at 11.30 am. You can see how very little was actually being done. So the first thing I did was look at how we structured the working day.

The second issue was the team dynamic: a couple of union reps were creating a pretty toxic environment. As both were coming to the end of their career and were never going to change, I removed them both from the rig without shaming them in the process. I then brought in some new team players, people I knew were real 'doers'. They would go out, do the job, and then come back and say "What's next?" It completely changed the team dynamic.

I also implemented a reward system. It was a very simple one, but it worked. I had some T-shirts designed with Shearwater and Shell badges on them. If you did something extra for the platform, you got a T-shirt. People then started coming to me saying, "Hey, look, I saw John and Tony wearing those Shearwater T-shirts. Can I have one?".

"Well, what have you done for the platform?" I'd ask. "When you've done something great, come back and see me."

It worked. If you didn't have a Shearwater T-shirt you didn't feel part of the team.

Understanding the dynamics of stressed individuals

Submariners have to learn to live together in an exceptionally confined space. On a Trafalgar class submarine like *Turbulent*, that space is just over 85 metres long, almost 10 metres wide and 9.5 metres in height. Inside this steel cocoon, over a hundred people spend weeks at a time, without so much as a glimpse of daylight, cut off from communication with their families.

Space is limited, personal space even more so — your possessions (books, family photos etc) are pared to the absolute minimum. You have less personal space than a prisoner. It's cramped and claustrophobic with many of the crew hot-bunking between shifts. You see the same people every day, work with them every day, eat the same food and sleep right next to each other. Officers and men live and work in the same conditions. (Only the captain has a separate cabin, adjacent to the Control Room but this is also small.) And on top of this, you live under the constant threat of attack, fire or drowning. The pressure can seriously take its toll.

Here's a scenario you could find yourself in on Perisher. I designed it deliberately to test a student captain's skill when it came to handling a seriously stressed-out individual. I timed it to coincide with a strike operations task, ramping up the pressure.

Taking a hostage during strike operations

You know before you start Perisher, you'll be sleep-deprived. It's to test your character. But you're now three weeks into the sea phase of the course and you haven't slept for more than four hours at a stretch. You're exhausted. Your body aches from the constant stress and sleep deprivation. You know there are times in command when you won't be able to sleep for long periods, so you have to get used to it. What you haven't quite got used to is the way Teacher will suddenly throw in the unexpected.

It's your turn in the Captain's Chair during a task for which you were given notice and for which you've prepared when suddenly an announcement is made over the main broadcast system. A young sailor has flipped out. He's locked himself into the Wireless Telegraphy (W/T) Room and taken one of the W/T operators hostage. He's now threatening to wreck the equipment in there with a wrench.

You know all eyes are on you, including Teacher's. How will you deal with this situation without jeopardising today's task? It's your job to negotiate with this sailor and keep the crew focused which is no easy feat when he then decides to broadcast rock music at full blast over the submarine's internal speakers.

You find out what his demands are: ice creams for the entire crew and a line through to his mum's phone so he can talk to her. What will you do? You need to talk him down and get him out of that room fast to prevent any further disruption to the crew. You have strike operations to conduct and he's preventing it. If you don't achieve them, the impact could be catastrophic.

I chose this young sailor for his acting talent and, unbeknown to the Perisher students, had secretly primed him to throw a wobbler at a certain time. His performance was worthy of an Oscar. It took the student an hour and a half to talk him down and get him out of the W/T Room. Ideally, of course, you want to minimise the risk of a situation like this arising at all. That means learning to spot the signs of stress early on and understanding the dynamics of individuals when stressed. It will help you navigate these situations and respond appropriately.

Stress has an interesting effect on people. While everyone experiences it, the way individuals react to it is unique. Some people become quiet and withdrawn, others may appear agitated and unable to focus, and some become aggressive. To recognise the signs of stress in your team, you need to know each individual well. If you don't, you won't be able to make a judgement call based on their normal behaviour. For example, if someone who's typically outspoken and gregarious starts to display atypical behaviour by withdrawing and isolating themselves, it may be a sign of stress and a cause for concern. The first step is to become aware of the signs and adjust your approach accordingly.

Next, practice empathy and active listening. Someone who's stressed may feel overwhelmed and have difficulty expressing themselves. By acknowledging their feelings and actively listening you'll be providing a safe, supportive environment. Empathy involves putting yourself in their shoes and recognising the emotional impact of the situation. If you can show empathy, you'll build trust and rapport which will help diffuse things. Overall, understanding the dynamics of individuals under stress requires close observation, active listening, empathy and — above all — patience.

Losing the team

Having earned a team's trust, you want to do your utmost to keep it. If you lose the team, it's hard to regain them. Should this happen, the first thing to do is acknowledge your mistake and take responsibility. Express genuine remorse for any damage you've caused, avoid excuses or blame-shifting and be transparent with the team.

Show consistency in action and word. If you promised to fix an issue, follow up and actively work towards a solution. Keep the team abreast of progress and inform them of any important decisions, changes or developments. Encourage them to ask questions and provide their thoughts on decisions that impact them. Showing leadership qualities centred around openness and consistency will eventually rebuild trust but it takes time, effort and commitment.

Pressure points:

- To lead well you must know the people you're leading.
- Lead by example. Keep a positive attitude. Always. Optimism is as infectious as pessimism.
- Prove yourself capable of driving or fighting the submarine once, then let them do it. Your most important success metric is measured by the generation you empower.
- Understand when team dynamics shift and act. If you have to isolate do it with compassion.
- Spotting and reading micro-expressions is invaluable when assessing a team's buy-in. Micro-expressions are involuntary; they can't be faked.
- Understanding the dynamics of stress requires close observation, active listening, empathy and — above all — patience
- If you lose the team it's hard to regain their trust.

Chasing the enemy's tail

HMS *Triumph*. Course 290 Speed 6Kt.
Depth 60M. Patrol Quiet state. Weapon Readiness State 2.
Area: Northern Fleet Exercise Areas. Chartered Depth:
950M. 1310 ZULU.
Captain has conduct. You are the Duty Commanding Officer.

At depth, and at slow speed, you could be alongside — you wouldn't know the difference. The crew is either carrying out its watch-keeping duties or relaxing or sleeping. On 1 Deck, in the Control Room, the Ship Control Team is driving the submarine under the orders of the Officer of the Watch. The Sonar operators are listening and analysing screens, searching for ships, submarines, fishing vessels, and biological noise and passing that information through to Tactical Systems operators who compile the tactical picture to enable decision-making. One operator is sitting at the Weapon Control Console, reading a manual. The Navigator is standing by the navigation plot ensuring that predicted positional information is available to the Officer of the Watch.

Towards the back of the Control Room is the Captain's cabin, a small, 9 x 3 x 6 ft compartment where you can just about stand up straight. The Captain is the only man with his own cabin, the drawback being that it's in the Control Room and on the passageway that leads to the Tunnel going over the reactor compartment. Opposite his cabin is what's known as the 'WT Shack' (Wireless Telephony) an historic name for the communications compartment.

The Captain's cabin is a little like a camper van. There's a wooden desktop that lifts up to reveal a sink below it and the sofa doubles as a single bed. As well as a sonar screen, there's a communications unit which allows him to listen to the constant exchange of information between all positions, if he wants. Things can happen fast on a submarine so this is not to check up on his crew, it's so the Captain will have situational awareness beforehand if he's needed in the Control Room.

The Captain and 'Teacher' have a special relationship. He and his crew are providing the platform for Teacher to train and assess future submarine captains. Despite the fact it is training, there is huge risk involved. A number of submarines have suffered incidents during this training — some of them were significant. In 2003, HMS Trafalgar, operating deep in the Minches (confined waters near the Shetland Isles) hit an island at 15 knots, resulting in considerable damage to the submarine and both Captain and Teacher being court-martialed.

The Captain is very aware of this, and ultimately the crew and the submarine are his responsibility. He knows Teacher well. They've worked together before and he trusts him. His crew received training before they started this course, but they have to a be a crew to 6 different student captains as well as Teacher when required. That concerns him. The crew will get tired, they will get consumed by the wartime exercise scenario and that's when things happen. He's the backstop to keep the submarine safe.

You're sitting in the Captain's chair looking intently at the 'Command Display', a series of screens showing a variety of data: navigation information, own boat information and weapon information. You've had it set to the best settings for Anti-Submarine Warfare (ASW).

Although submarines move relatively slowly when searching because modern submarines are so quiet, you don't detect them if they're very far away and they don't detect you either. The time you have to respond is therefore minimal. Decisions must be taken in seconds — minutes at best — and you must also assimilate information really quickly. You remember doing ASW training in the simulator, but this is very different. The entire team in the Control Room — the Sonar operators, tactical operators, navigation team and Ship Control team — are all working together to search for the other submarine. And that's only one part of it. There are Marine Engineers in the Manouevering Room and in the engine room keeping propulsion going and then of course there's the other watch, the remaining half of the submarine crew who are resting or preparing for the next watch. The sheer number of people involved in this operation; it's incredible, you think, looking around. It's a huge responsibility.

You look at the screen in front of you. Something is going to happen, but when? Stepping out of your seat you go over to the Warship Electronic Chart Display and Information System (WECDIS) to talk to the Navigator.

"Navigator, how are we doing with area constraints?"

"Duty Captain, we remain depth restricted to the deep zone – the nearest column of water with unrestricted is—"

His report is cut short as new information suddenly comes over the action communications:

"Ops Controller, new contact bearing 320," the Underwater Controller reports.

"Controller Ops, cut through — that's contact 211," says the Tactical Systems Operator.

You head back to your seat. Here we go, you think.

"Ops Controller, Contact 211 possible submarine contact, dangerous contact, close quarters bearing 330."

Over the main broadcast Ship Control Officer Watch pipes "Close Quarters bearing 330."

"Officer of the Watch, bring the weapon system to weapon readiness state one", you say from the Captain's Chair.

"FCO, Duty Captain, standby Spearfish attack against track 211 classified submarine." The order is repeated back and preparations begin.

Teacher enters the Control Room from the Captain's cabin. He comes to stand next to you but says nothing. You look at the Control Room – the team is functioning well.

Then, within 45 seconds, the Fire Control Officer reports: "Duty Captain, Weapons System Ready for Spearfish attach on track 211."

There's no time for you to think, you just need to do this. "Standby to Fire track 211," you say, and as soon as you hear "Weapon System ready'" your voice firm and strong, you give the order: "Fire".

The pressure inside the submarine as the Water Ram Discharge system operates, firing a huge slug of water, means people have to clear their ears. This is the simulated discharge of a torpedo. The other submarine will hear it and should respond by counter-firing.

Both you and Teacher watch the sonar screen as the 'enemy' submarine continues to go past very quickly. You need to get behind it to maintain tactical control. If it stays in your 'stern arcs' — a sonar blind spot — you'll have no idea what it's doing.

"Ship Control, Port twenty-five steer zero four zero," you say, and Ship Control acknowledges. You feel *Triumph* start to bank as it turns to start chasing the 'enemy's' tail. You keep your eyes fixed on the sonar screen, waiting to regain contact with the other submarine. Teacher is watching it too.

"So Duty Captain, are you safe? Have you avoided counter-detection? Are you achieving your aim?"

"I am depth separated," you reply. "I think we've been detected but not counter-detected and yes I'm still achieving my aim'."

You feel Teacher's eyes on your face as the reports keep coming in. The Ship Control team is trying to manoeuvre but as they turn, the submarine is stalling and that means it's sinking. They report in metres:

"5 deep, 6 deep, 7 deep — request more speed, Sir."

You're still watching the sonar screen. The noise level in the Control Room is increasing. Everyone is relaying information at the same time and each person is trying to talk above the other, believing their piece of information is important.

Now the Captain enters the Control Room. He walks over, looks at the navigation picture and watches Ship Control.

Teacher speaks again. "What's most important here?'"

Looking over at Ship Control you suddenly realise..."Sh*t", you say under your breath. "Ship Control, half ahead, revolutions four zero". The revs start coming on, then the next report is: "Ops Controller, we're cavitating".

You've lost control. You haven't re-detected the enemy, but at least you haven't been attacked. Maybe you've got away with it, but if you have, it was through luck, not judgement.

As the Ship Control team gains control and get *Triumph* back on depth, you hear "Ops Controller, Oscar Oscar Whisky (submarine attack) bearing 180". You've been attacked.

Teacher looks at you. "Once you've handed the submarine back, we need to go through this."

"Roger Sir". You regain control and then give the Officer of the Watch some direction and guidance.

As soon as he says, "I have the Submarine," you head a couple of decks down to the Ships Inertial Navigation Systems (SINS) compartment.

During this Perisher, the tiny SINS compartment on 3 Deck is serving as the student captains' office. Space is at a premium but the crew has made a makeshift table in there so they can do their planning. When you open the door, Teacher and the other student captains are already in there. You're all tired and these debriefs take up time. There are no chairs and only a couple of places it's possible to sit down. You walk in and lean against an equipment rack.

"So," Teacher says, "Take us all through your thinking. This course is all about learning from each other."

As you begin to relay your thought process, the other student captains listen. Some make notes. Having asked you questions about your thinking in forensic detail, Teacher says, "You had no authorisation. You've been detected and attacked. You haven't recorded any of your thought process or shared with anyone why you were doing it and you've lost control of the submarine while doing it. I don't understand your thinking, and I don't think the team does either. You've fallen into the trap of getting the first attack in. That might be right in an exercise, but as I've said, you've got to treat this a war. I get that no plan survives first contact with the enemy, but you must have a plan and options. You're lucky this is an exercise and not a real op."

CHAPTER 4

Know Your Enemy

'I think that most people would rather face the light of a
real enemy than the darkness of their imagined fears.'

Max Brooks, *World War Z*

'To know your enemy, you must become your enemy', the great
philosopher and military strategist, Sun Tzu advises in *The Art of
War*.[11]. His advice holds today and not just in warfare. In business,
you can't go against the competition without understanding them.
That means knowing everything there is to know about the people
involved — their capabilities, their strengths and their weaknesses,
as well as what motivates them.

To get to know his enemy, Field Marshal Bernard Law Montgomery
hung portraits of Nazi generals — including a signed photograph of
his nemesis, Erwin Rommel, — on the walls of his caravan. In the
late summer of 1942, as Rommel's Afrika Korps continued to press
against El Alamein, 'Monty' is said to have spent hours staring at this
picture, asking himself what would be going on in Rommel's mind.
It worked. In October he defeated Rommel in a battle hailed as one
of the turning points in the Second World War.

So, why would *you* need to know your enemy? What purpose does
it serve outside of war, in business? It's a major multiplier in strength
and influence. At best it gives you an edge; at worst it will at least
equal up the odds. But in order to be successful against an enemy,
you must know where and when to attack and where and when *not* to.

---

[11] Sun Tzu, *The Art of War*, Arcturus, 2020.

Imagination is important, it allows you to get into your opponent's mind to work out how to outwit them. Those who understand the value of knowing your enemy, also know it takes time to research. To *really* understand what makes them tick, you need to know their history, culture, philosophy and politics. Why? Because if you don't comprehend their history, it's difficult to understand their present — the now. If you don't understand their philosophy and politics (with as much intelligence as you can get) you won't be able to figure out their motivation — or how far they will go. And if you don't understand an organisation's culture – you won't know how to interact with it.

You'd probably expect anyone in the military to be an expert at this. But battles and wars fought in the 21st Century tell a different story at every level. For this reason, I adapted Perisher to better reflect the warfare landscape the Submarine Service was operating in and it continues to evolve.

Submarine captains in particular have a difficult task to ensure they're fully prepared because having sailed, once radio silent, all they have to go on is what they've researched in advance. Those leaders who are effective, realise time is short and start researching the enemy as early as possible. They know attention to detail is paramount. They also avoid dogmatism.

Threat evaluation

If you only know a 'platform' you never really win – you need to know the people who are fighting from that particular platform. When I was in the navy, I would spend ages reading the history of a nation so that I understood the background, the 'why' they were as they were. Russians are a case in point — they are hard people in general and that's created by their history.

In the military, the time you have before an operation is the only time you have to gather information without any distractions. The more you can gather, the better you'll know your enemy and the environment you're operating in. (This is also the planning stage of an operation which I'll cover in more detail in the next chapter.)

By understanding an adversary's capabilities, intentions and movements, military commanders can develop effective strategies to counter their actions and gain a strategic advantage in battle. It's also imperative you understand the context in which you and the enemy are operating.

Know the context

In his book, *Seamless Leadership*, Adriaan Groenewald writes:

'I have met some boring individuals with limited charisma or people skills who simply managed to take one step at a time in their business or corporate career to eventually reach a high level of success, but they did it with disciplined consistency. Then I've also met some very charismatic individuals with all the people skills that one can only dream of, but they jumped around from one opportunity to the next and never settled down into a rhythm of disciplined consistency and therefore never reached their full potential'.[12]

Context is important. It drives how anyone operates and equally how you lead. Knowing what you can control, what you can influence and what you can't, makes you realise where the boundaries are and where you can focus.

When a submarine is conducting operations, one key element of understanding how an enemy is operating is the context. The geography you are both operating in; what is happening politically; what is happening militarily; religions; people involved. There's

---

[12] Adriaan Groenewald, *Seamless Leadership*, Jonathan Ball Publishers 2015, p184.

that great moment in *The Hunt for Red October* when the Russians send ships and submarines to catch Ramius when they realise he's going to defect. The US takes that surge of military firepower as a potential threat and begins to counter it. The US doesn't understand the context (he's trying to defect); the Russians haven't anticipated the consequences of their actions.

During Perisher, I spent much time focusing on the context, based on my and other captains' experience. Having the right understanding, meant you could make better decisions, and take the right actions, position the submarine correctly, take the right level of risk because you could relate to the opposition's actions.

The only way to do this was to use the United Kingdom landmass (the simulators and at-sea training would be around it) to create new countries, politics, personalities, military capability and sometimes even languages, to give the students opportunities to operate within context. It was painstaking but enjoyable. The team I was working with took great delight in developing the personalities in particular! The simulator staff would operate the enemy really effectively, moving the students away from a mechanistic response, to strategically considered decision-making.

They could be gathering intelligence, or they could be preparing for special forces operations or other missions, but the context would drive some of the decisions they made. For example, if they were in a more passive regime, or pitted against a less capable enemy, they might push harder to gain intelligence, because of the risk of detection, and the consequence of counter-detection would be less severe than if they were up against a very capable and aggressive enemy wanting to exert regional supremacy. The impact of being detected by the latter enemy-type, in that type of situation, could be considerable in strategic terms.

It's similar in the business world. Understanding the context in which a business is operating is important, particularly if you're making decisions that impact customers or clients. However, understanding the context *within* a business, particularly for corporates, also deserves your attention.

I'll give you an example. I was once in a meeting where a large group of people, seated around an equally large table were attempting to find a solution to a problem. There were two groups from two different departments (planning and delivery) and the problem's impact was being felt across both departments.

The person presenting was under enormous pressure and constantly being challenged about why they hadn't completed the task and when we could expect it to be completed, in order to manage expectations. The conversation then became circular. The question kept being asked and the answer kept being given — a delay of about four weeks. Yet the leader of the delivery group kept coming back to the same question.

At that point, a potential solution presented itself to me. It would take a few days to resolve and need collaboration but, frustrated with the circular discussion, I jumped in and offered it, pledging my personal support to help achieve it. The Chair of the meeting agreed with my approach.

My boss, however, did not look happy and during a conversation afterwards, he asked me why I would offer to help them out. I explained that by doing so, we would achieve a 'win-win' for our company. It wasn't important which group solved the problem, as long as the outcome was successful.

He had a different perspective. The risk of not being able to deliver the solution could affect our group's reputation, he said, adding, "It's not even our problem. And if it's successful, they'll take all the credit".

"For my education, why is that important to you?" I asked.

"It's really important the CEO knows who's actually done this. When we get into the political piece of positioning ourselves within the company, these things count".

I may not have understood my boss's motives, but I now understood the context of his decision-making. It also gave me an insight into elements of that organisation's culture.

Understanding the context

The context will define how you plan, decide and lead. Spending time to understand it and apply it is another factor in managing dynamic situations everywhere. If you're able to focus on this with discipline, it will help you as a leader.

The definition of context is important. It's defined as 'The situation in which something exists or happens, and can help explain it.' In order to understand the context you have to spend time understanding the environment and be able to recognise pattern shifts.

In the military, those pattern shifts give you an indication that something may or may not be about to happen. At that point, you either deploy a pre-planned response, refine a pre-planned response, create a response, or do nothing. And sometimes, doing nothing is the best thing to do, as long as you understand the consequences of doing nothing or responding too late.

Similarly, in the business world, understanding what your competitors are doing is an important part of strategic planning. By monitoring industry trends, competitive positioning, and customer preferences, you can identify potential threats and develop effective strategies to stay ahead of the competition.

The 'enemy' may differ in corporate life, but the approach is similar. There are three initial questions you need answers to:

1. What is the enemy doing, and why?
2. What is the enemy's intent?
3. What are the enemy's patterns of life?

What is the enemy doing, and why?

To evaluate the threat, you need to assess the enemy's capability and potential. What is the enemy doing, and why are they doing it? You can spend too much time thinking about this but spend too little and you will almost certainly fail. In business, competitor analysis will help you figure this out:

- What products are they offering that you're not? Why?
- What's their target market and why?
- Why would your audience buy from them and not you?
- What's their pricing level? Do they offer perks? Why?
- What keywords are they going after and why?
- Which social channels are they using to market their products or service? Why?

The 'why' is vital. But as well as answering this question each time, you should take note of what's working for your competitors and what's not — and why. This will pinpoint their strengths and weaknesses as well as highlight your own.

For example, does your rival regularly get into slanging matches with customers on social media? Take a look at their customer service and Trustpilot reviews — is this an area where you can do better and gain an advantage over them? Why are they doing this poorly? Are they so well-established they're taking customers for granted? It could potentially be an opportunity for you to win them for your business. And what better way to find out more about a competitor's weaknesses than talking to customers who made the switch?

Poor online reviews can be useful for finding weak spots in a competitor's offering. But if a rival's getting good reviews, scrutinise these too. What's not being mentioned? Why?

Even a basic strengths, weaknesses, opportunities and threats (SWOT) analysis of each of your competitors can identify their strengths and weaknesses and highlight your own. But there are other competitive intelligence tactics you can use to dig deeper. Tracking personnel changes will tell you where the company is focussing resources and where it's not. Is there a pattern? A sudden exodus of staff or the disbanding of an entire department may be worth a closer look.

Do you keep abreast of industry news and developments? How well do your competitors know it? This speaks to understanding the environment in which you're operating. Knowing it better than they do, gives you an advantage and is something you can leverage to gain a strategic advantage.

Most submarines have a 'stern arc or baffle', a sonar blind spot, right behind at the stern. That means the best way to win a submarine duel without being detected is to get in behind your opponent before you fire. Knowing this weakness is all very well. But you have to remember the enemy knows it's one you share.

To manoeuvre yourself into a position where you can take advantage of this weakness requires strategy. And an effective strategy is borne from knowing your enemy inside out, what they're doing and why. Armed with that knowledge, you'll be in a better position to predict their movements, out-manoeuvre them and take them unaware.

What is the enemy's intent

In submarine combat, establishing enemy intent is arguably the most important factor. Operated by a team with the intent to attack or defend at all costs, even the least-capable submarine can be a formidable adversary. It can even prove a difficult target with which to engage effectively if you're constrained by your own rules of engagement.

Most people make the mistake of focusing on capability. That will get you into trouble. Without gauging their intent, an enemy's capability is pretty irrelevant. Pit a well-run, ancient diesel submarine against a nuclear sub operated by a merely capable team and the old one might win. This is even more likely if the ancient sub is operating in its own environment. I know this for a fact as I've been in exactly that position early in my career. It's a lesson learned that stood me in good stead. I've treated every adversary with respect ever since — an attitude which has undoubtedly put me at an advantage.

In business, establishing a competitor's intent is equally important. By analysing a rival company's intent, you'll gain insight into their strategy, long-term goals and objectives, target markets and marketing tactics. Determining these will help you anticipate their actions and plan strategic moves to compete effectively in the market.

For example, a competitor may have the capability to rapidly develop and launch new products. However, if they intend to undercut pricing and undermine your sales, you may need to modify your pricing strategy to stay competitive in the market.

One way of determining competitor intent is to look closely at their branding and marketing messages. Identifying common themes and value propositions will give you insight into their objectives (as well as their target audience). Monitor their social media platforms to see if there are trends or patterns in their messaging and engagement with potential and existing customers. You could also research their industry involvement paying attention to association memberships and participation in events.

What are the enemy's patterns of life?

In the military, understanding 'patterns of life' is crucial for success. Patterns of life are the routines, or habits of individuals or groups of people in a particular geographic location. Understanding these means painstaking human intelligence gathering by observing and analysing patterns in behaviour, movement and activity of the threat over time. The intelligence gathered will not only give you insight, it'll also help you determine the best time to carry out an operation with minimal risk to troops.

Human intelligence gathering (HUMINT) is the oldest method for collecting information about a foreign power and for most governments, despite the technological revolution of the late 20th century, it's still the primary source of intelligence.

Let's say you're the 32-year-old director of a rival start-up and my contact of interest. I'd start by finding out everything there is to know about the company you run, your motivation for starting it and your family background. I'd find out that you get up at 7.00 am, go for a run before work and arrive in the office by 8.30 am Monday through Friday.

On Tuesdays, you play Badminton after work with your best mate from 6 till 7.30 pm. Otherwise, you work late, before going home to your family at 7.30 pm — except on Fridays when you go out to a bar with your mates. And so this pattern continues...until it alters. And that's when I need to pay attention. Not the first time it changes — that's just an anomaly — it's the second time that's key. The second time you play Badminton on Thursday evening instead of Tuesday — when you go to a meeting — that's when I need to watch closely. Your threat level was based on a particular standard course of action. That was the norm and established a baseline. This change means I need to analyse and reassess, adjust my strategy and plan accordingly.

In the corporate world, gathering intelligence on a competitor's behaviour and routine allows you to anticipate their moves, identify opportunities and develop a more comprehensive strategy to stay competitive in the market. Careful observation over time will help you identify gaps or underserved areas in the market you can exploit. You may be able to develop a specialised product or service to fill this gap.

You might notice a change in behaviour that suggests they're planning to launch a new product or service. Now you can prepare a counter strategy to maintain market share. Monitoring competitor routines can help you understand their pricing strategy. You can then come up with a competitive pricing plan to stay ahead of them.

Every battle strategy is based, to some extent, on beliefs about what your enemy is likely to do. Understanding patterns of life can be tough, especially if you assume your enemy operates the way you do. Don't make assumptions.

Identifying the enemy

The enemy is not always who you think it is. On a submarine patrol, there are days full of action and excitement and days where you do nothing at all. On quiet days, you get through the boredom by reminding yourself of the exhilarating ones. The first time I encountered this was in 1994 when I was watch leader for the Dutch Navy. Four weeks of patrolling the Caribbean picking up drug smugglers and reporting as they transported their illicit products from manufacturers and growers to users proved tedious in the extreme. Patrolling makes it sound as if we moved around. The reality was we stayed in the same position gathering intelligence which was clearly being collected for good reason — however because of stringent security, we had no idea what that reason was.

The real challenge, I quickly worked out, was keeping motivated during this period. It's natural for people to slip into routines in these situations. In fact, in the cramped conditions of a submarine, when the only way to work out if it's morning or night is by the food you're being served, routine becomes your reason for existing. My way of coping with the monotony was to create a routine for myself. As watch leader, I always made sure I was prepared for the next watch. The rest of the time I filled with physical training — sometimes at the expense of sleep. Nevertheless, by sticking to my routine I was able to work with energy and enthusiasm.

Fast forward to April 2011 when I was captain of *Turbulent* and I was reminded of that Caribbean patrol as we made a fast transit towards Libya. When you transit underwater below 200 metres day and night feel the same: all the lights are on, the crew is going about its business and you feel little movement of the boat. Only when the submarine needs to manoeuvre do you get a sense you're getting somewhere. Otherwise, you'll only know what distance you've covered by looking at the chart. Most of our time was spent deep, returning to PD once every 18 hours to make sure we collected all HQ's messages.

To make sure we'd be ready for any eventuality when we entered the theatre, we ran drills. I was pleased to see the team was motivated, and working professionally and effectively. It gave me confidence that when the time came, we'd be well-prepared. However, until we were East of Suez, we were to conduct surveillance operations off the Libyan coast. Our instructions were to integrate into NATO's operation as part of the UK's support of military intervention in Libya.

Just before we'd started our sprint to the Mediterranean, there was a change to the crew. Luckily, as most of the new crew members had completed Operational Sea Training (OST), it was relatively easy to integrate them. To get through the Straits of Gibraltar (STROG) we had to surface, but once we were through we dived again as fast as we could. A submarine is always much more vulnerable on the surface. It's hard for other vessels to see us as only a third of the submarine shows above the waterline, so there's a greater risk of damage or collision, and it's more difficult to manoeuvre. It was a relief to get back to our natural environment — the deep.

Although we'd collected more communication on our way through STROG, we still had very little instruction about what we would actually be doing off the Libyan coast. The OST we'd received meant we were prepared for the worst-case scenario, but as by then Gadaffi's forces had been pretty much obliterated, we were concentrating on one particular area of warfare. Where we were going we'd be doing surveillance, reconnaissance, intelligence gathering and analysis, special forces operations, anti-submarine warfare, anti-surface warfare, strike operations and more. As we deployed to the next theatre of operations, we needed to up our game. Fast.

We already had a plan for this tasking which took into account what the enemy was doing and how we could achieve the best results. We'd also considered the geographical areas we'd be entering. As we arrived in theatre, there were already many NATO submarines operating there, enabling us to close the coast, and although this posed a degree of risk from our friendly forces, it was great training.

As we were there to deliver hostility to the enemy, the possibility we might use our Tomahawks was under debate by the crew. The less-experienced submariners were naturally fairly gung-ho on the subject. Others were clearly concerned about the moral implications. "We just need to get on and do it," I said. "When the time comes it will be my call and my responsibility. To support that, you need to concentrate on delivery." I had more pressing concerns in the shape of the first of what would turn out to be a number of challenges caused by our legendary but somewhat elderly submarine.

Turbulent's motto 'Turbulenta Hostibus Fiat' means 'troublesome to our enemies' and since her launch in December 1982, she'd lived up to it. She would be decommissioned soon, but the responsibility to complete operations despite her age was mine. Despite undergoing major maintenance before I took command, she was beginning to struggle and since then had required repairs. It was becoming a daily challenge to keep her going.

Our first setback off the Libyan coast was the reactor drive motor handle coming off. This was frustrating, as we'd changed the old handle before we left the UK. Now it seemed the new one didn't work.

The second and more urgent problem involved Tomahawk. The port-side weapon discharge system kept failing, meaning only three of the five tubes were available. That needed sorting immediately so we could fire our weapons. But this also meant we had a short-term problem for the crew. While the team carried out repairs, those men living in the (Weapon Storage Compartment) WSC had to hot-bunk in the forward bunk space. I loathed it when my crew were inconvenienced like this. To perform effectively, they needed to be well-rested.

Then, to cap it all, two more problems suddenly arose, one after the other. I was reading a book on the Middle East in my cabin when Dan Seager, the assistant marine engineering officer appeared.

"Sir, the garbo [garbage ejector] is not functioning."

This was frustrating, but as the crew were always watching my reaction and behaviour, I deliberately kept my voice even. "OK, be more specific."

"The garbo is blocked by a piece of string and will not shut properly to drain down."

We both knew what this meant. Someone had decided to take a shortcut by disposing of items which shouldn't have gone into the garbo and in trying to rectify their mistake had made things worse, resulting in a loss of capability.

Trying to find out who the culprit was and sanction them would just waste time. The best thing to do was accept it and move on. But moments later, Dan reappeared. Now we had a blockage in the slop pipework.

Individually, neither of these problems was serious. Together, they were disastrous.

When there's a blockage in the slop pipework, the Garbage Ejector (GE) takes over to get rid of waste. With both out-of-action and 130 crew on board, conditions would quickly become intolerable. We couldn't use the galley, sinks or washing facilities and had no way of getting rid of our waste.

I was not happy. I knew complacency had caused this situation. The moment you get comfortable you get caught out. It took over twelve hours to fix the GE and slop system and required a team of five engineers to painstakingly check metres and metres of pipework, drilling into pipes to check their condition, and then repairing them. Sixty man hours were wasted — all because someone had become complacent, taken things for granted and grown careless.

The situation hadn't defeated us (defeat on board *Turbs* was never an option) but it was extremely unpleasant to live in those conditions for as long as we were forced to. And it could have been avoided. While we were focusing our attention on Libyan forces, we'd ignored the greatest enemy of all: our own complacency.

On Perisher, you can get quite comfortable during the three months' training. But there's no room for complacency at sea when you're in the Captain's Chair. To test you, Teacher will constantly throw a spanner in the works. Sometimes literally.

Your own worst enemy

Sun Tzu's famous quote, "Know your enemy and know yourself and you shall not fear the results of one hundred battles,"[13] is

---

[13] Sun Tzu, *The Art of War*, Arcturus, 2020.

overused for good reason. However, it's rarely put into practice. Are you unknowingly your own worst enemy? Are you working against yourself, your team and your mission?

Successful leaders who endure are invariably highly self-aware and know their strengths and weakness (in both their personal and professional lives). But as I explained in Chapter Two, self-awareness is an ongoing process — a process of self-examination you should continue throughout your leadership journey. Before you pit yourself against an enemy, certain — after exhaustive research — you have a strategy which will exploit their weaknesses, ensure you're aware of your own.

On Perisher, you learn an incredible amount about yourself as your limits are tested under pressure. Your weaknesses are exposed in front of an audience — the entire crew. Sometimes you're fighting internally with your own emotions and at the same time, wrestling with others' emotions to keep them focussed.

In a warfare situation, you need to show aggression. Dithering won't do. A nuclear-powered submarine is a sports car, not a station wagon.

"What's the difference between your submarine commanders and the British?" a group of ex-submariner Russia-watchers was asked.

"Balls," they replied, without missing a beat.

During a Perisher course I was observing before I became Teacher, a student captain was being indecisive, appearing really weak and 'wet'. A sailor was sent to fetch a raw steak from the Galley.

"You need some red meat. Decide!", Teacher said, foisting the steak on the student. This protein moment was a first in Perisher's history, as far as I'm aware, and it's not a technique civilian HRs would use. But the student was getting lots of hassle and it lightened the mood — as well as having the desired effect.

Self-sabotage takes many forms: those energy-sapping thoughts that limit your vision and deflate you. Yet you're in control of these. You can shut down the naysayers in your head and refuse to let them work against you. In other words, don't make them your enemies and let yourself be defeated by them. Equally, avoid jeopardising your team's success by allowing yourself to surrender to that other arch-enemy: ego.

Be honest with yourself. Take a long hard look at the enemies within yourself you face. If you're to gain ground and avoid being defeated by them, you need to know them intimately. Awareness is half the battle. Ask yourself:

- How many times a day do you make excuses or blame others for a subpar performance?
- How often do negative thoughts get the better of you?
- Are your expectations of yourself unrealistic?
- Do you constantly find yourself repeating old patterns without working to find solutions?
- Do you give up too easily? If so, why?

Your mindset is critical to achieving your mission. When facing poor results, a strong leader doesn't give up or find someone or something else to blame. Failure is on you. It's why you make sure you're properly prepared physically and mentally long before you even face your enemy on the battlefield. And you assume they will be too.

The enemy within

You'll struggle to outdo your competitors if you don't know either yourself or your organisation from within. In the world of business, countless external threats can damage your organisation's chances of success, from competitive pressures to economic downturns. One of the most insidious dangers, though, is often overlooked — the enemy within.

In larger organisations, you may have more enemies than you realise. They come in various guises — internal politics, toxic cultures, and rogue employees, to name a few. So how do you identify and combat them? Because your competitors, remember, may well know about this weakness and be ready to exploit it.

Identifying an enemy within your team

Employees can be a company's largest resource. They can also be a liability. As much as you'd like to think everyone on your team is working towards the same goal, the reality is some employees may be hindering this.

Identifying an enemy like this can be difficult but it's a critical step in maintaining your team's high performance. I covered ways to spot when the team dynamic is shifting in Chapter 3 and how to deal with it. Here are some signs you may have an employee who's operating against your team's interests:

- They repeatedly refuse to work collaboratively
- They badmouth you or other team members behind their backs
- They make critical decisions without looping in other team members
- They belittle or ridicule their colleagues' ideas
- They consistently miss deadlines or deliver subpar work
- They don't show initiative to contribute to the team's objectives.

Any one of these signs could indicate an employee is working against the team. If you can spot this behaviour early and address it proactively you'll limit the disruption it can cause.

The bigger issue is the perception of threat some leaders feel personally from within their team. You need to accept that there will always be people who are better than you in your team. They are not a threat, they are there to be nurtured; they are our legacy. To allow space for others to grow, you should always be prepared to move on.

Identifying a toxic culture

Toxic cultures and internal politics can be a major enemy of any organisation. There are several signs you may be dealing with one.

1. High employee turnover rates: If high numbers of employees are leaving your company after a short time, it could be a sign they're unhappy with the company culture.
2. Lack of trust: If employees don't trust each other or their managers, it creates a negative work environment and can lead to conflicts.
3. Gossip and negative rumours: If there are a lot of rumours and gossip floating around the office, it could be a sign of a toxic culture where employees don't have open communication channels.
4. Micromanagement and lack of autonomy: If managers are constantly micromanaging employees and not giving them the freedom to make decisions or take risks, it can create a negative work environment.
5. Lack of accountability: When employees know there are no consequences for poor performance, it can create a culture of complacency and lack of motivation.
6. Blame-shifting: When things go wrong, employees or managers shift the blame onto someone else instead of taking responsibility.

Pressure points:

- You can't go up against the competition without understanding them.
- Know the enemy. It's not always obvious.
- Capability is irrelevant. Focus on enemy intent.
- Know the context. It defines how you plan, decide and lead.
- Be properly prepared. Assume they will be.

Joint Warrior

HMS *Triumph*. Course 010 Speed 3Kt.
Depth: 17M (periscope depth).
Patrol Quiet state. Weapon Readiness State 2.
Area: Hebrides North. Chartered Depth: 115M. 1410 ZULU.
Captain has conduct. You are the Duty Commanding Officer.

You're about to take part in a 'Joint Warrior' NATO exercise involving many warships, aircraft, marines and troops. For this exercise, the UK and Ireland are the 'Wallian Archipelago', the waters off Scotland's west coast a Middle Eastern flashpoint.[14]

What's creating this flashpoint is a country called Pastonia. Its borders are similar but not identical to Scotland — it runs across the south from Ayr in the west to south of Berwick upon Tweed in the east. South of Pastonia is Dragonia (its borders run from just north of St David's in Wales to Grimsby in the east, on the North Sea's coast). South of Dragonia is Avalonia. Northern and southern Ireland is now Ryania (named after Teacher, perhaps, but not confirmed).

There's a civil war in Pastonia, the consequences of which are concerning NATO countries in Western Europe. Pastonia is breaking up into two territories. One territory is controlled by the Government of Pastonia (GOP) which is based in Glasgow. The other is controlled by the far-left Peoples' Republic of Pastonia (PRP) whose headquarters are in Edinburgh (although Edinburgh Castle, which housed the PRP's Ministry of Defence has already been destroyed).

The GOP is still internationally recognised as the authority, but the PRP is trying to destabilise neighbouring Dragonia by funding and supporting the Free Dragonian Brotherhood, a far-left terrorist

---

[14] See map in the appendix.

group active throughout the Wallian Archipelago. The epi-centre of the civil war is the Western Isles, Isles of Arran, Cumbrae and Skye, where the Free Dragonian Brotherhood also has terrorist cells.

You've known about this exercise and the tasks required in advance and have been given time to prepare. You've got a handle on the environment in which both you and the enemy will be operating — the Wallian Archipelago is pretty similar to the Straits of Hormuz. You've gathered as much intel as you can. You've read books on the countries, their history, culture and people. You understand what's motivating them and how far they'll go.

It's the first time in your career you can't ask someone else what to do. A week ago, Teacher may have put a hand on the tiller to guide you. This week, you're on your own. He'll step in only if you make a mistake and that could end your Perisher. It'll be your turn soon, so you go back to your books while there's still time.

The tasking you've been given is reactive – a signal was received four hours ago that tasked you to transit as rapidly as possibly into the Northern Fleet Exercise Areas to intercept a potentially hostile task force. HQ has cleared water space from other friendly vessels for you to transit through and you're at speed.

The problem is the intelligence is vague: all it says is 'a task force'. This situation is really complex – there are many factions and many countries involved. If you get this wrong, you could have a negative impact on the overall strategy.

You're in O group, the daily operations briefing, and the team is discussing the strategy, plan and tactics to be deployed. The Intelligence Officer is pointing to a chart and talking about the potential units involved and you're wondering how you're going to deal with them. Which one of the ships and submarines involved could have the most impact on you conducting reconnaissance and intelligence gathering?

You've realised that if you're detected by any of the three countries forces involved in this brewing conflict, it's likely to start a sequence of events that could have catastrophic political impact. It could escalate the situation dramatically.

You know the team has been briefing the capability of the units involved, what types of sonars they have, the crew sizes, the radars, the weapons they use (including ranges and warhead size,) and the impact these could have on the submarine, but what they're not talking about is the tactics the enemy employs. What they do they look like? How we would see them?

They've concluded that the SSN (the United States Navy which is also involved in the exercise) is the real opposition – they're operating in the same space as we are and have similar equipment. The differentiator in all of this is the crew.

"What do we know about the crew and how long they've operated together?" you ask.

"Duty Captain," the Navigator replies, " I've been to sea on one of those boats for a few weeks. I don't know this particular captain, but I can tell you about watch-keeping cycles for the crew, how they operate as a team in the Control Room, the quality of their training and how they make decisions."

"That's great intel." You smile and nod at him. "So here's my first question. Do we understand their OODA Loop from initial contact to determining that they are going to attack, can you talk us through that?" The OODA Loop is a four-step process developed by US Air Force Colonel John Boyd. It stands for 'Observe, Orient, Decide and Act' and was designed to help fighter pilots make rational decisions under pressure, in confusing or chaotic situations.

The young officer talks through the process: what they do and how fast/slow it is. Teasing out more intel through questions it appears there are a few weaknesses you can exploit. What's more there are many strengths the 'enemy' has that you'll need to avoid.

Teacher interjects. "Duty Captain, I normally let you and the team carry on with this and the approach, but I would be remiss if I didn't share that I know the captain well. We served together when

I was on exchange with the US Navy. I've been to sea with him and know him and his family. What do you want to know?"

You and others start asking a variety of questions about the US captain to form an opinion. This is going to impact the plan, you realise. You don't want to fear the opposition team, but you do want to respect them.

The question is, have you identified the true enemy?

CHAPTER 5

Plan

'Everyone has a plan until they get punched in the mouth.'[15]

Mike Tyson

In *Maverick*, the latest Top Gun movie, Admiral Simpson (played by Jon Hamm) reminds Captain Pete 'Maverick' Mitchell (Tom Cruise) of his responsibilities as an SFTI[16] instructor training the best of the best for a potentially lethal mission.

"You have less than 3 weeks to teach them to fight as a team and how to hit the target."

"And come home." Maverick adds. "And come home, sir."

He's right. In submarine combat too, your mission doesn't end until you've got the boat and its crew home safely. That's why submarine crews don't just sail off and carry out operations. We plan, prepare and rehearse. We invest in training, when we're not on operations and we're not authorised to do operations until we've proven we meet the right level.

Leading in war doesn't provide the space for indecision. All that proactive preparation is key to avoiding reactive decision-making: the continuous training to hone skills and teamwork; to see people at their worst; to see yourself at your worst — and survive. Enabling people to achieve their best is vital. All the skill sets specialist professionals have

---

[15] When asked by a reporter in 1997 if he was worried about Evander Holyfield's fight plan, Mike Tyson is said to have replied 'Everyone has a plan until they get punched in the mouth'.

[16] TOPGUN's official name is the Navy Strike Fighter Tactics Instructor program or SFTI, for short.

acquired will pay off eventually … unless you're captured. In that situation, the emotion that goes with pain is considerable, although ultimately you will gain some form of control over it.

"By failing to prepare, you are preparing to fail", said Benjamin Franklin. Wise words indeed and often quoted in business books and blogs as a result. But for me, Napoleon Bonaparte puts his finger more accurately on the point of preparation. "If I always appear prepared," he said, "it is because before entering an undertaking, I have meditated long and have foreseen what might occur. It is not genius that reveals to me suddenly and secretly what I should do in circumstances unexpected by others; it is thought and preparation."

No plan survives contact with the enemy — contingency is everything. This is why my most important rule for operational planning is 'always have an out'. However, there's a fine line between the required amount of planning and procrastination. Good, well-trained teams do lots of planning. So do good leaders. That's not because the teams can't do their own, it's so you have plenty of options. In my Perisher *Guide to Taking Command*, I gave student captains the following advice but it holds for leaders in general:

'On operations, you should be geared to catch the enemy out but alert to prevent the reverse happening. As captain of a submarine, you'll be the one in your team who is always looking ahead and who has the confidence, ability and experience to anticipate the most likely or successful route to achieve your tasking. Despite this, you must allow your team room to come up with solutions. Hear them out instead of stifling their initiative'.

'If everyone is thinking alike, somebody isn't thinking,' George S Patton reportedly said,[17] and on *Turbulent*, I was

---

[17] This quote is most often credited to General George S. Patton, Jr. (1885-1945). He might well have said it during one of his famous speeches to

always keen for my crew to challenge decisions before I made them, especially at the planning stage. I made it absolutely clear that as far as I was concerned we were a democracy, right up to the point the decision was made. From that moment, we went forward as one — until the situation changed, when we were once again a democracy.

Seven questions and warning order

Planning is about asking the right questions in the right order. The planning tool I used when Captain of *Turbulent* is my version of the Army's 'seven questions and warning order' I've seen work well. I first came across this model in 2002, when I was chatting to an army colleague in a bar in Helensburgh. In Faslane on *Joint Warrior*, an exercise which involved a myriad of UK and NATO forces, he'd seen our planning methods firsthand.

"You lot are really awkward with your planning," he said. "We use this tool called the seven questions. At the end of it, there's a warning order. That tells the team what's going to happen and when."

I was intrigued. I knew we needed something different so I asked him to show me how it worked.

It took a while, but the Royal Navy adopted the army's planning process just before I took command of *Turbulent*. Changing it slightly, they renamed it the 'Maritime Estimate'. However, to get the most out of it, I thought it best to use it in its original form, which in my opinion was more effective. In the world of submarines, where time is always in short supply and decisions are everything, I thought it would give us more breathing space.

---

his men before going into battle. However, Stanford University Professor Edward Krehbiel also used the phrase in 1919, before Patton became a public figure.

In essence, 'seven questions' is a template designed to help commanders in the field see how they fit into the bigger picture. Imagine you're Captain of a submarine and you've just received your orders from HQ. Whatever the orders are, you need to work on an internal plan to complement them. During a patrol in command — against an extremely capable enemy — I received orders I will always remember. From HQ came a one-line signal (which is what we call a message in the navy) saying "Move north at max speed — detail to follow". Naturally, we obeyed, taking the submarine deep (which meant we'd have no communication) and moving at maximum speed. But while we were doing that, I knew we needed to work out an internal plan so that the next time we were in a position to communicate, we'd have whatever information HQ needed — whether that was our understanding of the enemy, our weapon status, defects, personnel, endurance or assessment of the environment. Now this was not to outthink HQ, you understand, it was simply to add to and support their strategic plan.

I always use a similar planning process, because I find the steps work in pretty much any situation. The seven questions are pretty straightforward:

1. What is the enemy doing and why?
2. What have I been told to do and why?
3. What effect do I want to have on the enemy?
4. Where can I best accomplish each action?
5. What resources do I need to accomplish each action?
6. When and where do the actions take place in relation to each other?
7. What control measures do I need to impose?

In the appendix, you'll find a completed example of the seven questions planning tool we used during pre-deployment training to prepare for combat against a fictional enemy — GING (simulated by

NATO forces). But that shows you how this planning tool is used in the military. How does it translate to the business world?

Although the enemy is different, if you're trying to work out how your strategy will fit and support your company's business plan, the military's seven questions model is really useful. The framework will help you develop a comprehensive plan while by systematically considering factors such as objectives, resources and timelines, as well as potential risks and challenges. By addressing each question in turn, you'll end up with a clear understanding of what needs to be accomplished and how you'll achieve it.

It also encourages you to consider the interdependence between actions. This is critical if your team is to be successful in achieving your aims, helping you identify bottlenecks or obstacles so you can plan accordingly. Since leaving the Navy and applying this process to corporate planning, I've found it helps me make better-informed decisions, reduce risk and optimise the team's performance.

In business, you'd adapt the questions to something like this:

1. What are our competitors doing and why?
2. What have I been told to do and why?
3. What effect/outcomes do I want to have on the competition?
4. Where can I best achieve these effects/outcomes?
5. What resources do I need to complete each action?
6. When and where do these actions take place in relation to each other?
7. What control measures and/or governance do I need?

The first two questions are to ensure you know what your planning needs to address. As you'll remember from Chapter 4, it's essential you gather as much information as possible on your enemy, the landscape you'll be operating in and the tasks themselves. If you get this right, you'll be better equipped to make decisions when it comes to it, and your outcome successful. Your team needs to trust in your plan, after all, and they can only do that if they have enough information.

The five questions that follow are so you can be sure you have the procedures and resources in place to effect the plan.

Now let's take a look at how you might use these questions to plan in a little more detail.

1. What are our competitors doing and why?

In the military, this first question is about evaluating threat by assessing the enemy's capability and potential. To do that, you need to determine the enemy's intent and gather as much intelligence as you can about their patterns of life. In business, you'll use question one as a prompt to gather as much information as you can about your competitors.

As discussed in the previous chapter, competitor analysis will help you figure out a rival's strategy as well as its weaknesses and strengths. Monitoring 'patterns of life' will provide you with a baseline you can use to prepare for what you believe your competition is about to do and pre-empt or counter it. Real-time analysis is vital too. It'll enable you to adapt your plan and make the right decisions down the line.

2. What have I been told to do and why?

Understanding the rationale behind the tasks you've been assigned is critical to making informed decisions and prioritising workloads. If you understand the 'why' you can better align your efforts with the organisation's overall goals and objectives. It also helps you and your team see your contribution fits into the bigger picture.

Personally, I prefer really broad, vague direction. It gives me the opportunity to generate maverick options as well as a wide range of courses of action. But whatever direction you're given, it's down to you to work out how best to employ your team so that you maximise strengths and minimise weaknesses. And, while that may seem daunting on occasion, if you've correctly identified the 'enemy', and you know as much as you can about them as well as yourself, you can plan with confidence.

3. What effect/outcomes do I want to have on the competition?

The effect you'll want to have on your competitors will vary depending on the specific context or industry. Typically, the aim will be to gain a competitive edge over your rivals. You might be intending to disrupt the market by introducing new products or services, or you might be intending to improve customer service or implement an innovative marketing campaign. Whatever you're thinking of doing, you first need to establish what your intended outcome is.

4. Where can I best achieve these effects/outcomes?

Next, you need to identify the most effective locations or channels to achieve your desired outcomes. In the submarine world, this means understanding the environment in which you're operating. In military terms, the environment is what's known as a 'force multiplier'. Those who understand their environment can increase their capability against those who don't. The most capable submarine in the world can be undone by a less capable one with a greater understanding of its environment. The environment extends beyond the physical. It includes the political, strategic, operational and media among others. Good leaders take time to understand all the environments they work in and ensure they adapt what they do to suit it.

You should invest a serious chunk of time researching the environment so you, too, can create an advantage, or avoid doing anything that might detract from your end goal. This may involve analysing market trends, consumer behaviour and competitor activity so you can develop a more focused and targeted approach. If your desired outcome is to increase sales, you may need to determine the most effective channels to reach your target audience. If they're on social media platforms, then that's where you'll want to focus your marketing efforts instead of wasting time and money using traditional advertising methods.

5. What resources do I need to complete each action?

Identifying and securing the necessary resources is the next step. Will you require additional funding? Will the company need to invest in new equipment or hire more staff? If, for example, you're expanding into new markets, you may need to invest in research and development, hire specialised personnel, or secure funding for expansion.

6. When and where do these actions take place in relation to each other?

Now plan and coordinate the timing and sequence of tasks. Taking time to consider the interdependence between actions will help you develop a more efficient and effective project plan. This may include creating detailed project timelines, identifying potential bottlenecks and — crucially — establishing contingency plans to mitigate risks.

- Identify all the tasks involved. This will ensure no task is overlooked.
- Determine which tasks need to be completed before others can begin.
- Create a timeline outlining when each task needs to be done and in what order.
- Identify resource constraints. This means considering limitations on resources like time, budget or personnel which could affect the completion of certain tasks.
- Identify any external factors that could impact the project, such as market conditions, stakeholder expectations, and legal or compliance requirements.

Once you've got this far, spend time analysing the critical path. Are there potential obstacles or bottlenecks that could jeopardise or prevent the project's successful completion? To ensure the project stays on track, you should regularly review this and develop contingency plans if necessary.

7. What control measures/level of governance do I need?

To minimise risk, you may need to establish certain levels of governance or control measures. These could include monitoring systems, quality assurance processes, or communication channels to ensure all stakeholders are informed. For example, if your project means implementing new processes, then new company policies may have to be put in place to ensure uniformity and consistency across the organisation.

Without control measures in place, how will you know if you're achieving success or not? If you're not, you must be willing to revisit your plan and change, adapt or adjust it. It's also imperative you know when you need to peak and when you and the team can rest — this means you'll get sustainable performance.

Tailor your brief to your audience

When the plan is in place and decisions are made, it needs to be briefed. But unless you can clearly communicate what it is you and your team need to do, the project is almost certainly doomed to failure.

Effective communication is about the audience, not the speaker, and needs tailoring to each. It's not a case of one-size-fits-all. Work out who needs to know what, and when, then deliver the message appropriately. It'll take time and effort to brief your message effectively both upwards and to your team.

It's how you deal with it that counts

All your planning gives you and your team intellectual space. It gives you the ability to anticipate and think out of the box. In submarine combat, this can save lives. Remember, when things go wrong (and inevitably they will) it's how you deal with it that counts.

Off the coast of Tripoli, in 2011, not far from the Colonel (as the crew aboard *Turbulent* called Gadaffi) we'd spent so long studying his actions, we were by now intimately acquainted with his regime, tactics and forces. We were enjoying a lively debate about the man himself when the general alarm sounded.

"Emergency stations, emergency stations, hydraulic burst, hydraulic burst, hydraulic burst in the control room. Stand by to operate the ship's systems and watertight doors in hand control." The hydraulic systems managing the masts had failed. Immediately crewmembers began to move quickly but calmly to their emergency stations. The firefighting teams readied themselves while Attack BA (fast reaction firefighting teams) moved to the control room fast.

Masts are vital. Without them, submarines can't remain at Periscope Depth (PD) for long because of the increased risk of collision. The safest place for a submarine to be is deep. So as soon as we were sure there was no risk of fire breaking out, we went deep to repair the hydraulic system. We would no longer be able to communicate with HQ, but we had all the information we needed about the tactical situation. Having worked out the likelihood of a strike in the next two or three hours was less than 40%, it made sense to get on with repairing the system. I'd inform HQ of the decision I'd made afterwards. Even so, it was an uneasy couple of hours. What if the tactical situation changed in the meantime?

The team rose to the occasion as always and managed to repair the fault in 1.5 hours. Returning to PD we received the daily intent signal instructing us to remain in position and carry out intelligence gathering. The team refined their plan. This was now a smooth process borne from understanding how to plan operationally and continuous practice:

- information was received;
- the team assessed it;
- added it to the planning process;
- understood how we fitted into the overall strategy;
- briefed clearly;
- then executed the task.

Not long after, it was time for us to close the coast of Tripoli. We did so at speed. There was no anti-submarine warfare (ASW) risk and although we were entering a busy shipping environment, we were out of the standard merchant vessel transit routes. Scant fishing activity had been reported recently, for obvious reasons.

When we got close to the coast, as I'd expected, there was nothing interesting to report going on at Al Khum, the Colonel's naval base. As the days passed, we did little except report on the activity of the embargo runners — merchant vessels running arms to Benghazi. HQ appeared reticent about using Tomahawk. The RAF was running the operation, which meant flown missions were being used above other means. It was typical of the internal politics that always seem to go hand in hand with war. Frustrating as this was, I focused on the positives. The mission was giving us a chance to hone our skills before we arrived in the more complex theatre east of Suez.

After ten days we heard *Triumph* was on her way to relieve us, which meant we'd be returning to the Middle East to carry out our primary task. At 00.30 I was woken by the main broadcast system.

"Next on propulsion watch lay aft."

Thinking that did not sound good, I got up and headed straight for the Control Room. Crew members were already hurrying past, heading aft.

"Officer of the Watch, how are we doing?" I asked.

"Sir, they're lining up for single-sided operations. We're reduced to thirty revs while that's happening. Surface contact density is fine." As doing this would significantly reduce propulsion availability, I knew immediately something was badly wrong.

It turned out that a three-year-old flexible hose designed to last ten years had failed so badly that ten tonnes of water had flooded into the bilge. This was a major problem. Although *Turbulent* had a two-sided system and only one side had failed, if the other one failed this would impact on reactor operations. We'd have to shut it down. That left only secondary propulsion available and we would have to 'limp' out of the battlespace.

When I got to aft to take a look, it resembled something out of a maritime nightmare. There was water everywhere and the men trying to sort out the problem looked soaked, dirty and exhausted. They knew as well as I, that if we didn't find a solution to the problem and the other side of the system failed, we'd be stranded 12 miles off the coast of Libya with no reactor power, forced to rely solely on our emergency systems. Given the political situation, we were in a very serious position.

The best strategy, I decided, was to withdraw while we could, request new hoses and carry out repairs when they arrived. We had no hoses on board and even if we had, they would have been from the same batch as those that had failed, so they were likely to be faulty too. I discussed the situation with the Heads of Department (HODs). Until I actually made a decision, we were a democracy, after all.

"Sir, we need the hoses, but I know we can generate some bungs which will block the system and allow us to get full capability back," said Ben.

"That may be difficult to justify to HQ", Ian pointed out.

"There are two potential sources to get the parts we need," Gareth chipped in. "We could either go to Souda Bay in Crete which is 400 miles away to rendezvous with our supply people or get what we need from the variety of NATO assets currently around us."

We all thought the second option was by far the most attractive.

"Good discussion," I said. "Right, let's let HQ know both options. Tell them we will pursue our own repair while awaiting stores via the NATO route. Ben, keep your team focused on working the problem through. They've done well containing this. Now we need to recover from it."

HQ's response when it came, later that day, was not what I'd hoped for. Using NATO assets was deemed too taxing. They thought it would be easier to go slowly to Souda Bay. It would take us two days at least and for much of the transit, we'd still be in the launch area. While I found HQ's decision challenging, I knew I wouldn't have all of the strategic facts they would or what service politics were at play. The crew with the least information would find it hard to understand why, with all the units around us, we couldn't be provided with some flexible pipes. Messaging was everything — avoid the politics, focus on the decision that had been made and prepare for the next phase. It was vital to downplay speculation - it adds no value. The team leaders were briefed accordingly and we headed to Crete.

Meanwhile, the team, convinced their idea would work and it was worth doing just in case, carried on making the bung. After a slow journey, we arrived in Souda Bay and boxes of stores were loaded on board. Straightaway the crew went through the boxes to find the replacement hoses.

Shortly after, one of the junior engineering officers appeared on the bridge, some very thin hoses in his hands. "Can you believe it, sir? They're not in the consignment. These look like hoses for something else." It was hard to believe, but the hoses we desperately needed and the only reason for our two-day diversion, weren't in the consignment. Yet I wasn't surprised. Over the years I've learned to rely only on my own team and to always have a contingency.

HQ was told of the oversight and responded that we were to wait while the correct hoses were located. I opened up the casing so everyone could get up and enjoy some fresh air. Ben and his team came up briefly, then went down below to get back to bung-making. We waited. An hour passed and then another before I got a call saying the parts hadn't left the UK. Unbelievable.

Managing not to show any sign of the frustration I was feeling I relayed the information. "We need to use our own initiative," I said. "And right now, my money's on the marine engineering department's solution to the problem." My confidence in the team was well-placed. Yet again, working with limited resources in an extremely testing situation, they proved themselves. By dinner-time, they'd fixed the hose and soon we were underway again, heading back to our original position, off Tripoli.

Pressure points

- Planning is about asking the right questions
- No plan survives contact with the enemy — contingency is everything: always have an 'out'.
- Know when you need to peak and when you and the team can rest
- Plan, plan and plan — no planning is ever wasted, it's just sometimes not used.

Fire, fire, fire

HMS *Triumph*. Course: 180. Speed: 3Kt. Depth: 17M
(periscope depth).
Patrol Quiet state. Weapon Readiness State 2.
Clyde Exercise Areas. Chartered Depth: 60M. 1410 ZULU.
Captain has conduct. You are the Duty Commanding Officer.

The constant hum of the ventilation throughout a submarine
acts a bit like a comfort blanket. You worry when it stops because this
can mean several things, not all of them good. At best, it means the
Air Conditioning Space is being cleaned (which usually happens on
a Sunday). At worst, it signals the start of an emergency situation.

As the Captain, if you were sleeping when the ventilation went
off, you'll be up instantly and getting dressed, because if the General
Alarm sounds, you'll need to get into the Control Room fast. Not
to take control, because submariners are well trained and follow
emergency procedures, but to blend the tactical situation into the
strategy.

Today, the ventilation stops and the General Alarm sounds.

"Emergency Stations, Emergency Stations, Fire, Fire, Fire, Fire in
the Galley", comes over the main broadcast system. You head along 2
deck towards the ladder to 1 deck and the Control Room.

You're walking among crewmembers heading quickly to their
Emergency Station and the first response firefighters (Attack BA)
who are moving at purpose towards the Galley. People get out of their
way as two of the crew, with full breathing apparatus came down the
ladder from the Control Room to 2 Deck. Other crewmembers are
grabbing Emergency Breathing System (EBS) masks and heading
towards their station. Nobody — but nobody — gets in the way of the
firefighting effort.

The General Alarm sounds again followed by "Reactor Scram, Reactor Scram, Next on Propulsion Watch lay aft". As you enter the Control Room, you glance at the WECDIS screen to see the exact position of the submarine. The periscope is still manned and rotating. Everyone has their EBS on, the Ship Control Team is communicating to a variety of 'outstations', information is coming in over the Main Broadcast and there is smoke in the Control Room.

If there's a fire in the Forward part of the submarine, the smoke gets everywhere and really quickly, which is why everyone is using the EBS. The submarine service learned lessons after the explosion under the ice on board HMS Tireless in March 2006 when two sailors lost their lives, and changed its procedures. The tragedy and its recovery are legendary within the service.

You're sitting in the Captain's chair with your EBS mask on, when the Officer of the Watch, who has been intently watching the Ship Control team, turns to you and shouts through his EBS mask, "Sir, the submarine is safe, the nearest point of danger is Brodick Island at a range of two nautical miles. We've suffered a fire in the galley and a reactor scram. DCHQ have taken the fire. There are no threat radars and sonar has no warship contacts. The closest contact is track 545, bearing 180, range 6 thousand yards, classified as a fishing vessel".

As you are absorbing this report, the planesman calls out the depth. They are losing control of 'the bubble — the angle of the boat. The problem is, they have no power from the reactor and are reliant on the battery which can only provide a much slower speed. They are bringing water into the submarine to make it heavier which will help it get back on depth and they can do that quickly. What they can't do is pump the water out as quickly. This means, if the submarine gets too heavy, it will start sinking. The only way to control this is to increase the speed while you pump the water out. And because of the reactor scram, you don't have the capacity.

You have a lot to consider here. As you look at the multitude of screens in front of you, you have to filter out what information is important and what is not. The telephone just above your seat, bleeps four times. You pick it up. "Duty Captain", you say into the receiver, still watching the screens.

"Sir, DCHQ is closed up. Submarine is at emergency stations. Attack BA have been beaten back. Full Fearnought team are getting ready to fight the fire. There are no casualties reported."

You continue to process all this new information, aware that Teacher is at the back of the Control Room, observing. You know he and his team have spent months planning these exercises: getting ships, helicopters, Royal Marines and support craft in place to put you and your fellow student captains through your paces. Teacher knows what's going to happen — he has to. It's to test the student captains' limits and push them beyond those to discover what their real limits are. And although this feels real, it is training. It's tough to be sure, but it is still training.

Teacher needs to make sure safety is not compromised. You're pretty certain you're about to be tested further. Something else will be introduced into the mix to ramp up the pressure. You just don't know what.

"Ship Control, how long before the main engines are back online?" You shout through your EBS mask.

"Sir, it's another 10 minutes before we get double main engine drive," the Chief Petty Officer shouts back.

You look over towards the back of the control room at everyone standing 'sucking rubber' as they call being on EBS. "Navigator, how long before we need to gather the intel?" The Navigator doesn't get to answer.

"Danger danger danger, new racket active Bearing 010. Classified Blue Kestrel radar fitted to the Merlin". At this, the periscope watchkeeper steps back as the mast lowers. As it does so, he flicks up the handles. If they're out as it's lowered, they'll catch the mast well on the way down and that will damage the periscope operating system. Automatically, he starts his stopwatch.

"Look interval is four minutes based on an 18-knot warship' he says as he walks over to the Ops position to check that what he saw through the periscope is represented on the tactical screen.

"The fire is out, the fire is out. Atmosphere readings to DCHQ," comes over the main broadcast.

This doesn't mean it's over. They may need to ventilate the submarine to clear smoke using outside air and that takes time and risks detection. You run through your options in your head:

1. Continue the mission with the submarine in its current state.
2. Delay, and potentially miss the mission aim.
3. Withdraw to safety.

It's a tough call.

"Team, Duty Captain, hold reports," you say. "The situation is, we need to get in and gather the intelligence in Brodick Bay. A Merlin is in the area. The fire has been dealt with, we're awaiting atmosphere reports, propulsion is 10 minutes out. We are safe, the priority is to avoid counter detection. We've got time to get this under control and achieve the aim. That is all."

Teacher, who is not wearing EBS, walks through the Control Room, approaches you and says in a low voice, "Are you in control? What's your thought process now? Does this tie in with the plan?" Y

As you start explaining your thought process, Teacher listens, glancing occasionally at the sonar screen. Then he looks towards the back of the Control Room, catches the Captain's eye and nods. The Captain goes back to his cabin. You'll find out later, after the exercise, he's going to speak to the Manoeuvring Room to tell them to return power. The reactor scram was a simulation.

"Ship Control, Manoeuvring, Double Main Engine Drive available…" As the Engineering Officer of the Watch continues the dialogue with the Ship Control Officer of the Watch, the Sonar Controller speaks on the net:

"Ops, Controller, new contact bearing 210, two shafts, five blades, whine audible, probable warship."

The mast is still down, it has been for three long minutes. The Merlin will still be in the vicinity. "1 minute to all round look", announces the periscope watchkeeper. You have less than a minute to calculate mathematically whether to risk counter detection but put the mast up to check for the frigate and stay safe, leave the mast down which will increase the safety risk, or go deep.

"AC, do the All Round Look on search. Ops, neutralise all rackets and report Blue Kestrel'. You trust your AC, who is also a Perisher student. As the mast goes up, the AC knows he must get the All round look done in 30 seconds.

The control room is in silence – as he goes around. "Mark that Bearing 211, Type 23 frigate, ten thousand yards, ATB 15 Port," he shouts and continues around. Just as he reaches the end he shouts again: "That Bearing, lower search, Merlin, three thousand yards, ATB 90 Starboard going into the hover."

At that point, you realise you've got a real problem. The Merlin — one of the most capable ASW helicopters in the world — is about to 'go into the dip' — lower his sonar 2089 into water between the isle of Arran and HMS *Triumph*. Tactically, this is not a great place to be.

Your telephone handset beeps four times. You pick it up.

"Sir, it's the DCO (Damage Control Officer). The atmosphere is in spec, all equipment has been stowed, permission to fall out from Emergency Stations."

"Give an update first that there is a Type 23 in close proximity and a Merlin, and that attack teams are to remain closed up before you do," you reply.

"Roger sir."

Over the Main Broadcast, the DCO tells the Ship's Company what's going on and people start moving around the submarine, going back to their positions prior to the emergency. Many of them are returning to their 'rack' or bed in the forward part of the boat.

Now the Ship Control team starts losing control of the submarine as its 'trim' changes.

As you look around the Control Room, taking in all the visual information you notice Teacher is now talking quietly to the Captain at the back of the control room. The captain shakes his head during the conversation.

You know you need to do something, but you're thinking you want more information. The situation might change for the better. And sometimes doing nothing is the right thing to do.

"Transmissions watcher bearing 260 – classified 2089 – Helo is in the dip. Second set of Transmissions Watcher bearing 211 - classified 2050." Both the frigate and the helicopter are now aggressively searching for you.

- Do you wait?
- Do you push on and get the intel (take the risk)?
- Do you go deep and slow down?
- Do you go deep and sprint?
- Are any of these decisions right? Is none of these decisions right?
- Are there other options?

The time frame for a decision is collapsing. Your AC is saying something to you, suggesting something, but you can't hear it, your vision is narrowing as the pressure on you is increasing.

"Duty Captain, 1 minute to the all-round look." You glance over at Teacher and the Captain and note they're just observing.

As the mast goes up "Danger Danger Danger," is called out and the mast drops immediately as the AC steps back.

It's too late, you're no longer safe. "Officer of the Watch, take the submarine deep to 30 metres," As you hear all the orders, you check the submarine is going deep. This gives you another two minutes or so to decide.

- You could evade having not achieved the aim.
- You could evade and come back.

You're going to evade and come back. But is this the right call?

Charging Type 23 Frigate

Visit to the House of Lords

Examining the decision making of a student captain

Celebrating success

Frigate close

Duty captain under pressure

CHAPTER 6

Decide

'War is made up of risks, and a wise strategy is little more than an intelligent choice of risks.'

Bernard Brodie, *The Layman's Guide to Naval Strategy.*

Decision-making is a fundamentally human activity, even in the 21st century, when AI, machine learning and automation are becoming prominent. Leaders — strategic leaders in particular — are now faced with incredible open scrutiny of the decisions they make. In the military, this has always been the case, although it was generally done in private by a select group, as opposed to now, when everyone scrutinises decision-making.

Nelson said the most precious thing is being able to decide. He was right. Be indecisive, or decide too late, and you risk the safety of your crew. You could all perish. We'll discuss the decision-making process later in this chapter when we'll explore how much information you really need to make a decision, when is the last safe moment to make one, how to understand its impact, and how you learn to have the moral courage to make the right decision. First, we need to talk about risk.

Risk

According to the Association for Project Management, 'Risk analysis and risk management is a process that allows individual risk events and overall risk to be understood and managed proactively, optimising success by minimising threats and maximising opportunities and outcomes'.[18] It's a very broad definition. A simpler definition of risk is that it is ultimately a story of tragedy (or avoiding it).

A few years ago, I attended a seminar at the Scottish Police College given by Gordon Graham. Despite all the technology available to him, Graham presented using an old overhead projector, one laminate and a marker pen. He spoke solidly for four hours and his 'story of risk' was brilliant. According to Graham, risk is a study of tragedy. Everything that goes wrong has a story; when you look back, you can see the warning signs, the proximity event, and the tragedy.

He describes it as a three-step process:

- The proximity event
- The tragedy
- The litigation.

Risk management, therefore, is about avoiding tragedy, however small.

Risk is an overused axiom, talked about by many but understood by few. It's become the buzzword of the decade, probably because of decision-makers' concern that their actions are under constant scrutiny by those who don't have to make decisions on a regular basis. I suspect in many organisations those who determine how risk is managed rarely have to take risks themselves and therefore don't understand the personal element that is entwined within the process. You can formalise, mandate, regulate, scrutinise and criticise risk-taking, but unless you have taken proper risk with proper consequences yourself (and experienced those consequences) you can't *know* risk.

Having read many Board of Enquiries reports, I've discovered there are some common trends revealing the 'proximity' event or events. Whether it's decision-making, culture, the alignment of the

---

[18] Ruth Murray-Webster & Darren Dalcher, *APM Body of Knowledge*, Association of Project Management, 7th edition, 2019.

'Swiss Cheese model' or others. In some cases you see repetition. How did this happen twice? Why didn't they learn the lessons from the first event? Why didn't someone share this before?

Reflection on this was important. I analysed my own decision-making when I was in command. How did I make those decisions? Did I consciously manage risk? I know I took risks often. I did so because I knew my crew, our platform, our enemy and the environment. I also understood where the limits were. I understood the consequences if we were wrong. The impact militarily, politically, and reputationally was not always clear, but I was aware of it.

The recent *Titan* disaster is a tragedy that in the end came down to the poor decision-making of CEO Stockton Rush. He and four others on board the submersible lost their lives when it imploded last month during an underwater tour of the Titanic wreck. It was an unnecessary tragedy.

"You're remembered for the rules you break," Rush apparently said, quoting General Douglas MacArthur. "I've broken some rules. I think I've broken them with logic and good engineering behind me."[19]

An employee of OceanGate, the private company Rush founded in 2009 offering customers (or adventurers as he liked to call them) the chance to experience deep sea exploring, said he was passionate about what he was doing. And he was good at igniting that passion in his staff. Yet, despite the steep price tag of $250,000 (£195,000) for an underwater adventure, another junior employee said much of OceanGate's equipment had a home-made feel.[20] As well as using off-the-shelf electrical development boards instead of custom-designed ones used by other engineering companies, Rush is reported to have

[19] Stockton Rush quoted in LBC article: 'I've broken some rules", 22 June 2023. Available at: https://www.lbc.co.uk/news/ive-broken-some-rules-oceangate-titanic-submarine-window-pressure/. Accessed June 2023.
[20] OceanGate employees quoted in BBC article 'Titanic sub firm: A maverick, rule-breaking founder and a tragic end. Available at: bbc.co.uk/news/world-us-canada-66014565. Accessed June 2023.

driven the Titan with a game controller and used rusty lead pipes as ballast.

Rush's rule-breaking also included the use of carbon fibre with titanium end plates for the submersible's hull — materials used in the yachting and aviation industries successfully and largely untested in deep water but cheaper than industry standard steel. And instead of a spherical hull which means it receives an equal amount of pressure at every point, the Titan's was cylinder-shaped. To make matters worse, the plexiglass viewport installed so passengers (sorry, adventurers) could see out, was certified only to a depth of 1,300 metres which falls considerably short of the ocean floor where the Titanic lies at 3,800 metres.

Almost 4,000 metres down in the Atlantic is not a place you want to cut corners. Despite being warned of the risks of using an uncertified prototype in a hostile environment, Rush retorted that "safety was about culture, not paperwork" arguing that Titan's safety systems were state of the art, "way beyond" anything else currently used.[21]

In 2022, Rush told a journalist, "It really is a risk-reward question. I think I can do this safely by breaking the rules".[22] Well, it turns out he couldn't do it safely. Far from it. For Rush, the reward outweighed the risk.

"What is the lesson of *Titanic?*" filmmaker and director of *Titanic*, James Cameron said in an interview with *National Geographic*. "Heed the warnings. Do not let greed and arrogance supersede your best judgement. I mean, the captain of *Titanic* was highly seasoned, highly respected, and yet he didn't heed the warnings and he steamed full

---

[21] Stockton Rush quoted in BBC article 'Titanic sub firm: A maverick, rule-breaking founder and a tragic end. Available at: bbc.co.uk/news/world-us-canada-66014565. Accessed June 2023.

[22] Stockton Rush to CBS reporter David Pogue, 2022. Interview available at: https://www.cbsnews.com/news/titanic-submersible-interview-transcript-with-oceangate-ceo-stockton-rush/ Accessed June 2023.

speed into an ice field on a moonless night. And 1,500 lives were forfeited as a result. That's the lesson."[23]

The same could be said of Stockton Rush. He failed to heed the warnings, ignored the risks and let greed and arrogance supersede his best judgement. He refused to listen to anyone else and didn't involve anyone else in the decision. Five lives were forfeited as a result.

When I was interviewed about the tragedy on the news, I said all maritime activity has risks because the sea is unpredictable. That's why, before you take a submarine to sea you go through endless checks and training. I sincerely hope this form of 'extreme tourism' practised by OceanGate is now reined in. In any case, visits to the wreck of the *Titanic* should cease. It's a grave, after all. It should just be left alone.

Managing risk

How you manage risk is entirely dependent on how you understand risk. And the way you understand risk depends on your perspective: the perspective of someone who has to make decisions with impact; the perspective of someone who doesn't; the perspective of a risk-averse leader; and the perspective of a risk taker. Working with so many different organisations, I was able to see how individuals and teams dealt with risk and compare it with the Submarine Service. Initially, I concluded that the Submarine Service was much better than many organisations, but that discredited the context in which the risk was managed.

For example, managing the risk during a dynamic hostage-taking situation may not look the same as managing the risk of a construction programme falling behind because of potential supply

---

[23] James Cameron quoted in National Geographic, available online at: https://www.nationalgeographic.com/science/article/exclusive-titan-exploration-james-cameron-bob-ballard?loggedin=true&rnd=1688118381769 Accessed June 2023.

chain issues. Furthermore, you need to look at what develops risk aversion in organisations and that comes down to culture and personality. If a leader has had a bad experience or consequence after taking a risk, it will impact their subsequent decisions on risk.

During Perisher, you could see this with some of the captains whose submarines we were onboard. I was willing to let the students take more risks than the captain himself and when I had discussions with these captains as to why, it appeared to stem back to a causal event they did not want to repeat so they would avoid it altogether. This is an observation, not a criticism; it's the same in businesses too.

Most organisations talk about risk as a process, but because it's a human activity, there is an emotional side to risk that requires consideration. It makes you look at risk differently. When you do that, you learn how to accept the right level of risk to achieve results. This is not about filling in a risk assessment or managing a risk register – those instruments are sometimes blunt and while they collect data and may enable a conversation, they sometimes remove the constant consideration that is required with risk.

While training submarine captains, one of my tasks was to understand how each candidate perceived risk and how they managed that process. Could they justify the risk they were taking? What did they think the risk was? Did others see the same or other risks? It was evident that in something as fluid as warfare, risk is really difficult to manage. If you spend too long thinking about it, you can lose. And equally, if you don't spend long enough thinking about it, you can lose.

In developing the process, I was able to see the impact of risk on team dynamics and trust leadership. In a submarine, the leader has to make decisions in a time-deficit environment. In most cases, this means that risk is often not discussed, it's just the plan. The assumption is that whoever is making the decision has considered the risk and what might happen.

What submariners are very good at is asking 'what if?' They continually think about potential courses of events and attempt to have a tactic ready to deal with it.

"What if the submarine we're following turns around and comes straight towards us?'

"What if the enemy frigate starts transmitting on its sonar?"

Analysis of each of these potential situations allows you to develop a series of counter plans you could deploy almost immediately.

As you can imagine, for a submarine captain, decision-making is not simple. There are internal factors to take into account — a submarine is an extremely complex piece of engineering and you have people in it. There are external factors to take into account too, including the political situation, the environment you're operating in and how the enemy (or potential enemy) is operating. In addition, the quality of that information is variable. If you don't make the right decision, then you unlock a series of less controllable events — and the key during operations is to retain control. The paradigm is that in many cases you naturally feel you want more information to understand the risk and make a decision, but you're never going to get it.

There are a variety of methods of operational planning available for every level of command and operation that suit different organisations, units, teams and personalities. Whichever method you use, there are two decision inhibitors you must overcome.

The first is that the volume of information provided is significant. In this situation, the leader has to determine what is relevant and what is not. The second is whether the leader is concerned about the way their actions and plan will be perceived by those at a higher level. We've all seen the second and I expect many of us have experienced the feelings that go with that. When you are able to deal with both these decision inhibitors, the planning and execution process becomes significantly simpler.

Taking that information into account, if you can focus on three things, you can decide about risk and then work out how you are going to manage it. It then forces you to make a decision on the data that is present at the time.

The three elements involved in making the decision are:

- Time
- Information
- Outcome(s).

Time

Assuming that any decision you make will result in some form of action, you need to understand when that decision needs to be made. One of the first questions I would ask my team when I was being asked for a decision was "When do I need to make that decision?"

My reason (and I explained this) was that if it's a complex decision and there is some time available, then the pragmatic decision-maker will use that time. This discipline also avoids the impact of reactive, intuitive decisions.

Information

To make decisions you need information. There are many different questions you can ask to obtain that information. In command, I would ask, "Tell me what you know and what you think you know and differentiate between the two." When decisions involve risk to life, they need to be correct. Fact and speculation can blur; intuition is not always a safeguard. It's safer — and quicker — to ask the question.

So how much information do you need to make a decision? The complexity of the situation that requires a decision determines some of this. In reality, it's dependent on the individual and the amount of training and experience they have.

The pandemic, while tragic for many, is an example of the effect of information and timing on decision-making. Some leaders acted on less information and the effect of that action, despite being unpopular, probably worked. Others waited for more and more information. Perhaps overwhelmed by the amount of information they received they found themselves almost paralysed by it. The impact of that paralysis was significant — it forced huge amounts of reactionary activity, creating now positive outcomes. The reasons why they did this will be beyond most of us, and only known by them.

Those of us who have planned and executed missions, albeit not at a national level, probably struggled to understand how decisions were made based on information and requirements. I considered this against how I would expect future submarine captains to engage in similar activities but at a tactical level. When you break it down, at every level, there are simple principles that work.

The challenge for every leader is to work out what is influencing their decision-making timeline. Some of the things they need to consider are not about the timeline itself, but their personal process. Once they understand their personal process, they can adapt that to the timeline, making sure the decision is made at the right time.

I'm convinced that this comes down to personality and training. Personally, I don't need too much information to make a decision. I know that in dynamic environments if I delay it will have an impact. While I'm mindful of the fact that 'decision/indecision=paralysis' I'm also aware that people need a decision to get action going. And the great thing about getting action going is, if something needs to change, you already have the momentum to effect this.

Outcomes

What is the particular outcome you want? Once you have decided, then it is time to transition that to action. Sounds pretty straightforward, doesn't it? The trouble is outcomes can be hard to define and as a result often end up being too vague.

Looking at your team and saying "we need to be better", isn't a clearly defined outcome. You need to be more specific:

- We want our team to become a highly driven meritocracy, all focused on the same goal, all underpinned by the right values.

- We want to exceed the Board's expectations on profitability. (Most companies want this.)
- We want to change from an R&D-focused organisation into a commercially focused one.

All of these are outcomes and within them, there will be objectives to get you there.

Justifying your decision (scrutiny)

I make decisions, but I want them to stand up to scrutiny. As a submarine captain, my decisions during a patrol were scrutinised by people who had one thing I didn't have: time. They could spend hours/days/weeks mulling over data to work out whether I'd made the right decision — sometimes I had, sometimes I hadn't.

At first, I didn't like this. I took it as criticism (there was some). "But you weren't there at the time," I'd say to myself. However, I quickly realised that when I removed my personal feelings from the equation I could be more objective and accept there may have been better decisions made. From then on, I was happy to have my decisions challenged and scrutinised. I still am, particularly if the outcome is wrong. It gives me the chance to learn and add the experience to my library of experiences I can draw from going forward.

The four pillars of risk

Corporates attempt to eliminate risk. However, because risk-taking is human — and humans are flawed, fallible beings — from the outset you need to accept you cannot remove all risks.

There are, in effect, four pillars of risk:

1. The people you lead

Everyone attempts to employ the best people, some organisations believe that everyone must want to be a leader (the military in particular), but if everyone is leading, no one will follow. You need a mixture of leaders and followers and you must reward both effectively. What is most important is that the people you have, buy into what you are trying to achieve. If they can't or won't buy into your vision, at some point they will impact your output in two ways:

Reputation — they represent you therefore whatever they do ineffectively is you being ineffective.

Destructive behaviour — if there are those who don't like being there, they can disrupt others and that becomes a cancer within any organisation. This is the most difficult pillar of risk to manage.

2. How you plan and achieve.

Sir John Harvey-Jones, Chairman of ICI, said that for those with no plan, failure comes as a complete surprise.[24] Those who are conscious in their planning, however unstructured, provide themselves with the best chance to reduce or remove risk. For some it's a natural process, for others it requires structure.

The military provides a variety of planning tools (one of which — 7 reasons — we explored in Chapter 5. Some are complicated, some simple. But it's not a case of one-size-fits-all when it comes to planning. Whichever tool you use, the key to dealing with this element of risk management is discipline. You must ensure you actually do plan, and have measures of effectiveness to determine if your plan is working (or not).

3. How you train (personally and as a team)

Those who train effectively are part of teams that build spare capacity into their thought and action process. This in turn minimises risk.

For example, submariners exercise as though they were at war, because when things go wrong, they go wrong quickly. Even in

---

[24] John Harvey-Jones, *Making it Happen: Reflections on Leadership*, Harper Collins, 1988.

peacetime, unless you recover the situation rapidly, the consequences could be fatal. You accept that the response during training may not be 100 per cent of what you would see in a real incident, but the process and techniques must be correct and if they are not, you must hone them constructively. How individuals train themselves is also a factor that reduces risk. By inculcating a culture of personal preparation, by example and encouragement, you increase corporate knowledge and skill. By increasing those, you reduce risk.

4. How you monitor

Leaders need to have some form of checks and controls to reduce risk. It is a delicate balance which only experience will manage. Many organisations, including the military, are becoming burdened by oversight, generally by those who don't have to take risks. The tendency to increase auditing, regulation, legislation and restriction only adds to the team's burden. There are many ways to oversee. In some cases, subtlety is key, while in others you need to be more direct. But you must have a structure.

How to develop the moral courage to make the right decision

'Few men are willing to brave the disapproval of their fellows, the censure of their colleagues, the wrath of their society. Moral courage is a rarer commodity than bravery in battle or great intelligence.'

Ernest Hemingway, *A Farewell to Arms.*

Decision-making is an art; making the right decision, however, requires moral courage. To my mind, moral courage is one of the essential characteristics of a good leader. Over the course of my career, I've come to recognise that someone's technical know-how or years of experience aren't as important as their honesty, ethics and moral courage. Submarine command tests both your physical and moral courage. I looked for both these character traits in student captains on Perisher. Now, when mentees ask me what makes a good leader, I will unhesitatingly answer moral courage (along with other attributes such as consistency I'll discuss in the next chapter).

Unfortunately, as Hemingway pointed out, moral courage is a rare commodity. Moreover, it's only recently begun to be recognised as a trait which is critical to strong leadership. The reason? Courage makes change possible.

Courageous leaders can effect significant change. But courage is not the same thing as bravery. Bravery is about doing what needs to be done even if it means putting yourself in harm's way. In the workplace, bravery is doing a task that scares others because you know it's vital to your firm's success. Or hiding your emotions and not letting them affect your interactions with colleagues when you're having a difficult time. Bravery may be a one-off. Courage, on the other hand, is an enduring quality.

The dictionary definition of courage is having the 'mental or moral strength to venture, persevere, and withstand danger, fear or difficulty.'[25] *Moral* courage is having the ability to do what's right — even when it might be unpopular or risky — instead of taking the safe or easy option. It means you'll speak out against injustices when no one else does; stand up for your beliefs in the face of criticism by others; and take action despite knowing it will personally cost you.

Moral courage requires a strong sense of personal integrity and a commitment to doing what's right. Even when it's challenging or unpopular. There are several reasons why it's a trait to be encouraged in leaders:

1. By making ethical decisions and taking responsibility for your actions, you demonstrate your commitment to transparency and accountability. That inspires trust and confidence in you. Not just among your team, but stakeholders and clients too.

---

[25] Merriam-Webster, online, accessed 23.5.23.

2. Holding yourself and others accountable for their actions promotes a culture of accountability within your organisation. You set clear expectations and standards and ensure everyone is aligned with the company's values and vision.

3. Even when there's uncertainty and resistance, having moral courage means you won't settle for "But we've always done it this way". You'll lead through change instead, taking calculated risks and pursuing innovative solutions. Leaders who can think outside the box and are not afraid to challenge the status quo can inspire creativity and drive innovation within an organisation.

Ultimately, as well as earning the respect of employees and stakeholders alike, leaders with moral courage are more effective at driving results and achieving goals. But while It's not necessarily innate in all of us, it can be developed.

First, you need to decide what you stand for by taking the time to define your personal values and beliefs. What's important to you? How do you want to live your life? Working this out will help guide your decision-making and give you a clear sense of purpose.

Second, you should practice self-awareness. As I said in Chapter 2, you must know yourself if you're to get the best from your people because how you operate influences the way others operate. But it's also essential to become aware of biases and fears you have that may influence your decision-making. By recognising and addressing these, you'll make more objective and ethical decisions.

You may want to seek out role models too. Look for people who demonstrate moral courage and closely observe the way they handle decision-making and difficult situations.

- How do they behave when providing honest feedback in discussions with partners, stakeholders or the board? Do they display humility as well as the courage of their convictions?

- Do they encourage team members to share alternative perspectives or opposite viewpoints?
- Do they take ownership when they're in uncharted waters and the safe option would be to do nothing?

As Ben Horowitz says, 'Every time you make the hard, correct decision you become a bit more courageous and every time you make the easy, wrong decision you become a bit more cowardly." If you're CEO, this has a knock-on effect. The choices you make will lead to a courageous or cowardly company.[26]

Practice speaking up. Start small by speaking up when you see something that goes against your beliefs and values. This could be as simple as voicing your opinion during a meeting or calling out a colleague you believe is behaving unethically.

It's vital you reflect on your experiences, though. So after standing up for what you believe in, take the time to do this. What went well? What do you think you could do differently in the future?

Pressure points:

- Risk management is about avoiding tragedy, however small
- Fact and speculation blur. When gathering information before making a decision, differentiate between what you know and what you think you know.
- Understand your personal process and adapt it to your decision-making timeline
- Decision-making is an art; making the right decision requires moral courage.

---

[26] Horowitz, Ben, *The Hard Thing about Hard Things*, *Harper Collins*, 2014, p.213.

Black ops

HMS *Triumph*. Course 290. Speed 3Kt.
Depth: 17M (periscope depth). Action Stations. Weapon
Readiness State 1.
Clyde Exercise Areas. Special Forces insertion. Chartered
Depth: 45M. 1910 ZULU.
Captain has conduct. You are the Duty Commanding Officer.

You're standing in the Control Room. As it's after sunset, it is in 'red lighting' so that the periscope watchkeeper's eyes are adjusted to the outside. It will soon be returned to 'black lighting' — complete darkness except for the lights on panels and dimmed-down tactical and navigational displays.

At night, in black lighting, if you come up from 2 Deck into the Control Room, you really can't see anything. But like all submariners, you carry a torch. Yours has a red filter to reduce eye fatigue, which comes in handy if you need to use it for long periods of time.

As you stand behind the navigation plot WECDIS, the Attack Coordinator has a massive checklist in front of him. You've always thought this was an unnecessarily complicated process, but you know it's proven and therefore you should follow it. You also know anecdotally that Teacher was never a fan and, in fact, adapted and simplified the process when he commanded his own submarine.

Earlier in the course, during the shore phase of training, you'd challenged Teacher about this.

"I justified my decision to alter the process because I knew my team well, they knew me and we all knew our boat. For Perisher's sea phase, there's no way you'll know the crew that quickly, so stick with the proven process," he said, adding, "When you're in command, you'll work out what achieves the aim best for you and your team."

Submarine services around the world carry out Special Forces (SF) insertion and extraction. Being able to enter an area undetected, launch a Special Forces team so they can undertake their mission and then recover them can give you an advantage over a potential enemy. The insertion and extraction process involves synchronising the whole submarine to make sure that the time spent exposed to potential detection is at an absolute minimum.

Today's Perisher exercise is to recover a special forces team post operations.

To simulate a typical scenario in which to test student captains, the West of Scotland has become a number of 'hostile nations', sometimes fighting amongst themselves and sometimes collaborating. The Isle of Arran is both a military and terrorist hotbed.

You're well aware there are at least two frigates operating in the area: one is a UK Type 23, and the other is a Dutch Zeven Provicien class. These concern you. They're both capable units, but the fact they're both carrying helicopters makes them even more of a threat. As Prestwick airport is not far away any ASW (Anti-submarine warfare) helicopters based there could be 'on top' very quickly too.

You weigh up the balance of risk. You know you need to recover the SF Team – if you don't, who knows what will happen to them if they are caught by the enemy. But you're also responsible for ensuring *Triumph* remains undetected so you don't come under attack.

The AC is standing nearby with his check sheet, and the submarine's XO is next to him, occasionally providing advice. "AC, Duty Captain. How are we doing with preparations?" you ask.

"We're good Sir," he replies. "We're at T-10 for readiness (10 minutes to go)".

You like the fact that whoever is taking their turn as Duty Captain is treated as if they were actually the captain by their fellow students, despite each of you being the same rank and all of you trainees.

"Officer of the Watch, Duty Captain. Tactical sitrep (situation report)", you say, looking at the young Officer of the Watch standing by the Ops position. After looking at all the positions, he reaches to his right and presses the 'Push to Talk' button on his remote headset.

"All positions, Officer of the Watch. Hold reports standby brief. We're currently 2.4 miles of the Isle of Arran, the submarine is safe in 45 metres of water, Special Forces have signalled for extract at 1930, Track 240 Type 23 is to the south of us at an estimated range of 10NM conducting an East-West patrol pattern. The other frigate is not held. No Airborne activity is evident. No neutral activity at present. We are 8 minutes from go/no-go decision. Priority is counter-detection and monitoring any change of the Type 23's Modus Operandi. End of brief. Standard reports."

After he finishes his brief, communications continue on the operations circuits.

"Ship Control, Officer of the Watch. Black lighting in the Control Room," a young officer on the periscope says and a few more lights are switched off in the Control Room.

By the tower — the access between the Control Room and the bridge — a young officer and a lookout are standing ready in their foul weather kit. At the back of the Control Room, the Casing party is ready. In the Engine Room, more of the casing party and many engineers are waiting to support.

You look around and clock Teacher coming out of the Sound Room towards you.

'Happy, Duty Captain?' Teacher asks.

"Yes Sir, all in control."

"Ops, Sonar. Possible zig Track 240," you hear over the communications net. "Transmission watcher, bearing 180 classified 2050 Type 23."

This alters the situation. The Type 23 Frigate is now transmitting on active sonar — searching for you. That doesn't mean it's found you, but it knows you're there. You already know there's a decision that's going to have to be made and it's either success within a collapsing timeframe or failure.

You decide to brief the team.

"Team, this is the Duty Captain. Despite the Type 23 frigate's change of tactics, we can still achieve the aim. We need to be quick. We'll continue to close the RV position and recover the SF team."

Teacher is now standing next to you. "So, you're going to close the position and carry out the recovery?"

"Yes, Sir."

"You're going to risk a £1 billion platform, a crew of 120 people, the tactical initiative and the political position to recover a team of 6 capable individuals who can look after themselves?"

As you ponder this, doubt starts to creep in. You've made the right decision…haven't you? But if you have, then why has Teacher questioned you over it? Should you trust your intuition? Maybe you've got this wrong. Teacher knows what he's doing after all. What have you missed? Without discussing anything with anyone, you start running alternative options through in your head. You pick up the handset.

"Team this is the Duty Captain. I assess the risk to be too great. We are going to abort this recovery. AC, contact the SF team and tell them to abort extraction, further instructions to follow."

Teacher hasn't moved. He's still standing beside you. "So, Captain, you're going to leave the SF team with the hostage they've recovered in hostile territory, knowing people are going to be looking for them. You're going to quit the mission you've been tasked with, just because you consider the risk too great?"

Now you're between a rock and a hard place. But then it dawns on you… you've missed the point. You need to learn to deal with challenges, justify your own decisions and stick to your course when you're sure it's right."

CHAPTER 7

Lead

'The first responsibility of a leader is to define reality. The last is to say thank you. In between, the leader is a servant.'

Max De Pree, former CEO of Hermann Miller, Inc.

In my privileged position as Perisher Teacher, I was able to objectively look at team dynamics, determine where challenges lay, and hopefully enable teams to realise and change them. In the majority of cases, leadership was at fault.

The dynamic and time-deficit environment in which submariners function requires exceptional teamwork and effective leadership. Perisher student captains need to stand out as a team *capable* of making difficult decisions and the individuals need to show that they *will* make difficult decisions. Decision-making is an invaluable skill, particularly when you know it has real consequences. However, despite being linked, leadership, followership and decision-making are three totally different tenets of success. You earn your privilege to lead, you must earn and give your followership if you are to lead successfully, and you must learn to make decisions.

We explored the art of decision-making in the previous chapter. We'll discuss followership in the next. In this chapter, we'll explore the elements that create strong leadership.

Leaders versus managers: what's the difference?

Before we go any further, let's be clear on the difference between leadership and management. Because there is a very definite distinction. Leadership is an art; management is a science.

Let me explain. Managers are process-focused. They control their team to execute the processes required to complete a task. Leaders, on the other hand, are people-focused. They inspire, empower and enable their team to achieve the common goal.

In the first chapter of *Leadership is an Art,* 'What is leadership?' Max de Pree says, 'The measure of leadership is not the quality of the head, but the tone of the body. The signs of outstanding leadership appear primarily among the followers. Are the followers reaching their potential? Are they learning? Serving? Do they achieve the required results? Do they change with grace? Manage conflict?'[27]

It's easy to tell the difference between a manager and a leader. Look at the team.

Leadership simplified

Having looked at leadership models across many different organisations, including the Navy, most seem to be unnecessarily complicated. My leadership model is simple.

Leadership - simplified

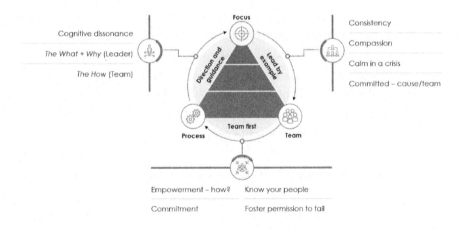

---

[27] Max de Pree, *Leadership is an Art,* Currency, 2004.

There are three elements:

1. How you provide focus
2. How you deal with your team
3. What processes you have in place.

And there are three ways to achieve this: leading by example; putting your team first; and direction and guidance.

1. Lead by example
   Leading by example is about the four Cs:

   • **Consistency**
   • **Compassion**
   • **Calm in a crisis**
   • **Commitment.**

Let's look at each of these one by one.

Consistency

Consistency means people know what to expect of you. Be consistent in all you do. If you say you're going to do something, follow through. Consistency also applies to your emotions. It's difficult to follow a leader whose behaviour is inconsistent because of mood swings, so keep your emotion in check. (I discussed how to do this in Chapter 2.) You're never too happy and never too sad, always somewhere in between.

Compassion

Compassionate leadership means being aware of others' needs, being non-judgemental when it comes to other people's perspectives and being tolerant and empathetic to people in distress. In this situation, make sure you show *real* compassion. People can tell when compassion isn't genuine so don't fake it. You'll end up making things worse.

Calm in a crisis

Stay calm in a crisis. If the leader's panicking, everyone else is going to panic more. If you remain calm, you'll be able to calm your team too.

There's a great scene in Apollo 13 when Jim Lovell (played by Tom Hanks) reports they're losing oxygen from the Odyssey. "Houston, we have a problem," he says and the noise level in the control room back in Houston rises as everyone starts to shout in their panic.

"Quiet down, people, quiet down," says Gene Krantz (played by Ed Harris) "Let's work this problem through". And everyone just calms down and starts doing exactly that.

Commitment

You must be fully committed both to your team and to the cause. Because if you're not committed to the cause, it'll come out at some point. You can lead, but you can't lead responsibly unless you're really committed to the cause you're dealing with — whether that is your firm's purpose or a particular task.

After all, if you're not committed to your vision, if you don't truly believe in it, how can you expect your team to buy into it?

So often, there's a disconnect between what a leader believes and what they're telling others to believe. You see this in corporates a lot. They'll have entire teams working on strategy, but go up to the CEO and say, "Hey John. What's our purpose?" and he won't be able to tell you.

The best way to illustrate this is to give you an example of an organisation where this is done well, where everyone is personally invested in the mission. At Fusion, if you ask anyone in the company "What are you doing?" they all say the same thing: "Solving the problem of fusion power with the simplest machine possible". That's complete buy-in to our firm's purpose. Underpinning this is that by achieving our goal, we're going to make a world worth inheriting.

2. Team first

Empowerment

Everyone talks about empowering your team, but few know how to achieve this. The only way you can empower your team is by knowing your people well so you understand what they're capable of. While you want to push them beyond their limits, you don't want to stretch them too far. Otherwise, they could fail catastrophically and that could be damaging.

The team needs to feel their leader is committed to them. You won't always get their commitment to you in return — that has to be earned. But you should be committed to the team itself.

Permission to fail

You should also foster permission to fail. At First Light Fusion, we fail all the time — as you'd expect when you're trying to solve the problem of fusion. In fact, we've deliberately cultivated a culture where we say it's alright to fail. I did the same on a submarine. I'd let the team know it's alright to fail, as long as you let us know so we can fix the problem. However, negligence, in the submarine service or the business world, is never acceptable.

3. Direction and guidance

Cognitive dissonance

Because you're a leader and because you're bright you can't be wrong, right? Wrong. Holding fast to this belief about yourself causes cognitive dissonance. And that, in turn, causes tension.

You see this in politics at the moment. Politicians are making some of the worst decisions possible, but they can't be wrong decisions because they all imagine themselves to be exceptionally bright people in positions of power and authority. Stockton Rush, the CEO of OceanGate is a classic example of this attitude too. The consequences of that kind of thinking speak for themselves.

The what and why

Giving direction means explaining the 'what' and the 'why'. Let's use Fusion as an example:

What: We're going to build an experimental machine called M4.

Why: Because it's a step towards building the pilot plant. And in order to build the pilot plant we must do this to prove we can get gain for Fusion.

The 'how' is for the team. You've explained what we're doing and why it needs to be done. Now it's down to the team to figure out how we do this, rather than you telling them. Of course, in the background, you'll work up your own, broad plan in case the team doesn't come up with one. Your plan doesn't need to go into detail though. You may not be a specialist in the field, after all, and you don't want to undermine the team by asking for their expert advice at this stage.

In the submarine service, if we were going off to do a patrol off the coast of Iran, for example, I would study everything about Iran because that's the way I operate. I'd figure out an outline of a plan but wait and see what the team came up with. If they were stumped, then without giving away my entire plan, I'd make a suggestion.

"Have you thought about this?" I'd say and give them a nugget. Something that may stimulate an idea they can run with and then pivot their thinking.

Learn to lead out of context

There are going to be times when you need to be able to lead out of context and make decisions in circumstances you have never encountered before. One of the changes I made to Perisher when I was Teacher, was to set up a 'leading out of context' experience where students swapped jobs with police officers. It was a way to introduce best practices from other command courses but it was also to teach students how context informs decision-making. Leading in a new situation makes understanding the power of context even more critical.

As a leader, how you deal with issues — rationally or irrationally, with confidence or without — and whether you control events or allow events to control you, provides an example to your team. Adapting Jeff Conklin's definitions of 'Wicked' and 'Tame' problems[28] is helpful when it comes to dealing with leadership challenges.

- **A tame problem** is one you have encountered before or one to which you can apply the principles of a previous solution.
- **A wicked problem** is one you have never come across before and are unable to solve based on past experience, forcing you to deal with it intellectually.

What we were faced with on patrol serving under Commander X (whose leadership style I discussed in Chapter 2) was a wicked problem — one that no one onboard had experienced before. It's at moments like these that strong, decisive leadership is needed most. But when things went wrong, instead of stepping in and taking charge of the submarine, Commander X let the Officer of the Watch manoeuvre the submarine without direction while he continually berated him, which only compounded the problem.

---

[28] Jeff Conklin, *Dialogue Mapping: Building Shared Understanding of Wicked Problems*, Wiley, October 2005.

Any ability to outthink the enemy was removed as he focused his fear on the next level down of leadership and they in turn focused on attempting to keep ahead of him. This pattern was repeated throughout the patrol until the submarine eventually returned to the UK. The effect onboard was that morale continued to diminish and the camaraderie element of leadership faded completely. Sanction — or the threat of sanction — gained primacy. And while *direction* was still understood to an extent, *example*, the most achievable of all the leadership elements within a submarine, was damaged beyond repair.

There is always a way to turn any negative experience into a positive one, however, and this captain gave me the best illustration of how not to lead. He taught me to rely on no one but delegate well, not to worry about others' perceptions and — most importantly — the value of *example* and how it has the most effect on success or failure. In the corporate world, there's an argument that 'hard management' is necessary to drive results in workplace culture. Having experienced this first-hand and witnessed its effects, I disagree. Instead, I leveraged this insight to serve my team in command and inform how I trained and assessed trainee submarine captains.

Once I'd left the navy, I found myself leading in several different contexts. A great example of this was Affinity Water. I hadn't long been with the company more than a couple of weeks when we had our first major incident. And there I was, Silver Commander, in charge of this incident with no real water knowledge.

Simply put, the reservoir level was dropping dramatically. It was in 2020, during the pandemic when we had a heat wave. There's no way of refilling a reservoir except to get tankers in from all over the country. In the meantime, how are you going to manage reservoir levels to make sure you can service your customers without resorting to 1000s of bottles of water? The only industry I know where people are happy it's raining is the water industry.

Very quickly, I realised that the decision-making process was causing problems. People weren't disciplined about the way they were relaying information; it was coming fast and furious and in terminology I'd never come across before. I realised we could fix part of the problem, but I needed people to change the way they provided the information. So I asked them to slow down, avoid industry jargon and acronyms and speak in a language I could understand.

Being the Chair of the Plymouth and Argyll Community Trust has also had its challenges. Although it's provided me with a great opportunity to learn from other leaders, it's a context I've never come across before and the skill sets required are different. It really is leading out of context. While I've coached CEOs of charities, I've never operated in the education sector and had very little training initially. Finding myself doing an Ofsted inspection, for example, put me way out of my comfort zone. What I did was draw from the skills I already have as a leader.

The other trustees are all subject matter experts in their particular areas. So if it's a safeguarding issue we have, there's an expert with the knowledge who can help inform a decision. The same goes for finance. The key to leading out of context, the real skill, is in enabling others and levering off their specialist knowledge to come up with a solution.

What leaders should avoid doing

So far, we've talked about what strong leadership involves. The 'dos' not the 'don'ts'. But there are things any leader should avoid doing, whatever the context. So here's a list of behaviours to avoid:

1. Micromanaging— it leads to resentment and a lack of trust. Instead, delegate tasks and responsibilities and allow team members to work autonomously. If you do need to jump in, it's important to make sure they know it's an intervention and not that you're trying to take control.
2. Being too controlling or rigid in your approach — it can stifle creativity and innovation and prevent team members from taking ownership of their work.

3. Showing bias or favouritism towards certain team members — it can create a toxic work environment and damage morale.
4. Refusing to take responsibility for mistakes or failures — it can erode trust and respect among your team and undermine your credibility.
5. Being inconsistent and allowing your emotions to surface and affect your reactions — it creates a climate of fear and reprisal which can diminish morale and damage your team's loyalty and respect.

Finally, remember that the temptation which confronts every leader is the same one which has brought many a dictator to a sticky end. 'Power corrupts' is a dictum that applies not only to politics and government. As a leader, your personality is accentuated. Avoid subjective leadership (which is all about you). No one should have to endure your temper, sarcasm, contempt, teasing or any other foible you develop. In any case, displays such as these only highlight your weaknesses. Candid and regular self-examination will keep you balanced and check any tendencies. And, if you do forget yourself, have the courage to apologise afterwards.

Objective Leadership

The captain I aspired to emulate was the one who gave me the most opportunity, John Richardson, the inspiring man I described in Chapter 3. John Richardson was an objective leader; nothing he did was to further his own career, he was all about his crew. From him, I gleaned a real insight into leadership and decision-making, as well as what motivates a team. Aside from John, I also learned a great deal from the ten captains I served with before taking command myself.

Of course, there are leaders who show a combination of both traits. But in my opinion, a successful submarine captain is an objective leader, one who sees the submarine through the eyes of the crew and empowers them so they can think for themselves and work together towards the common goal.

Empower but retain the ability to intervene at the right time

In the military, officers are meant to empower those lower down the ranks. In reality, this is not always the case. The services don't like those in power to show any sign they don't know something or might need to defer elsewhere. It most likely stems from the archaic perception that a leader should go charging into battle first. While this is undoubtedly sometimes necessary, it's not always required. As a result, those in higher ranks constantly scrutinise every tiny detail and micromanage each step which can end up frustrating and disempowering their teams.

If you don't delegate, your team members never learn to make decisions for themselves and enjoy the responsibility that comes with this. Since leaving the Submarine Service, I've seen firsthand how this transfers to the commercial arena. When I was at Shell on a high-temperature, high-pressure platform in the North Sea, it was difficult to begin with as I knew little about oil and gas. What I soon realised though, was how a lack of knowledge can empower your team to make decisions and get on with things. If my team needed me to make a decision, all I required was the relevant information and the options available. Then I could step in and make that decision.

To delegate effectively, however, it's vital you clearly communicate expectations and train and support people properly. Otherwise, they will struggle and that's destructive. Give them autonomy, but monitor progress by checking in regularly or asking for progress reports. In other words, delegate authority, not responsibility.

You should also retain the ability to intervene if it looks as though they're not on track. This might involve offering guidance or redirecting resources. Occasionally, it may mean making a difficult decision such as restructuring the team. But by striking the right balance between empowerment and intervention, you'll create a positive and productive environment and a team that feels valued, motivated and invested.

When I took over command of *Turbulent*, I was determined to provide objective leadership. I wanted to empower the crew to be the best team — not the best we could be, *the* best. To do this, I needed to create an environment in which success was theirs and failure mine and mine alone. From the outset, I made it clear that while mistakes were human, negligence was unacceptable. Maintaining our reputation was one thing; putting people's lives at risk was quite another.

Lives may not be at stake in your organisation, but an objective style of leadership is, in my opinion, what you should be aiming for. After all, you want good people in your team and smart people don't usually want to work for someone who doesn't have their best interests at heart. The best leaders make employees feel they care more about them than they do about themselves — because they do. And that inspires loyalty which is the next thing we need to talk about.

Loyalty is a two-way thing

Leaders who inspire real loyalty see their role as motivating, empowering and developing those they lead and they see their team as more than just people to help them achieve their own goals. Instead, they find meaning and purpose in bringing out the best in them. However, loyalty isn't a given. To be a leader truly worthy of loyalty requires hard work, self-examination and a clear objective. After all, who's going to follow someone who doesn't know where they're heading?

There are many ways to inspire loyalty, even in the most reluctant team members. If you're always looking over your employee's shoulder, second-guessing their work, for example, you'll create a sense of mistrust (especially if there's no reason to doubt their expertise).

Showing you trust and respect your team — without reservation — will motivate them to reciprocate.

Similarly, employees who are encouraged to develop their talents and perform over and above what they thought were their limits are more likely to feel loyalty to the leader who empowered them to do this. Employees in a workplace where there's no opportunity to develop and learn, on the other hand, may feel they're stagnating and become disenchanted and mistrustful. Another way to inspire loyalty is by demonstrating you'll never ask anyone to perform a task you're not willing to undertake yourself. If you expect your team to come in early and stay late, then you must do the same. Show you're in the trenches with them and you'll earn their respect.

In the military, a leader generally gets back a good deal more loyalty than he often deserves due to the inherent loyalty of officers and ratings to the system. But this should not blind him to the real meaning of the word which is often misconstrued by young or inexperienced team members. This means that as a leader, you must understand its true significance.

Loyalty is two-way. Loyalty upward is not enough; it should be bestowed equally on those above and below you. A leader who is disloyal to his people or who abdicates his responsibility instead of 'taking the weight', should expect an equal lack of loyalty from his team.

So what does a loyal leader look like?

- You give credit to your team for whatever they achieve
- You go the extra mile for them and roll up your sleeves to help
- You encourage two-way, open communication at all times
- You disregard previous mistakes
- You have your team's back.

In challenging times, the payback for this is that you and your team will show up for each other. Your team offers you their unswerving support because they know you'll always do the same for them. I know this because it was illustrated during one of the most challenging occasions in my own leadership journey.

Turbulent was the high point of my career in the submarine service, the moment when I could put all I'd gleaned from my experience and observations of other captains into practice. But it was during a 286-day deployment in the Indian Ocean, 237 of which were spent underwater, from which we very nearly didn't return, that all my leadership skills were tested to the utmost. A succession of challenges (many of which were a result of operating an ageing vessel in conditions it wasn't built for) altered my perceptions and refined my thinking about leadership.

I knew that to make the most of our people on that deployment I would need to be very aware of my own strengths and weaknesses as well as the team's. I did that and managed to create a strong team. Trust your people to use their talents and give them the freedom to do so and your trust will be rewarded: they will rise to the challenge. My crew certainly did. In fact, because of their success and achievements on this deployment, I was selected to teach Perisher. But if I'd been told that day we headed off on patrol from Fujairah might well have been my last, my farewells to my family at the airport the night before would have been somewhat different.

We were tasked with conducting an indication surveillance tracking and reconnaissance (ISTAR) patrol. These are demanding as you're dealing with potential enemies as well as friendly forces and trying to avoid both. If our submarine was detected we would fail and failure would undoubtedly have political consequences. Despite being in friendly territory in the United Arab Emirates, you could still feel the tension.

Even at 7 am, it was sweltering in Fujairah that morning, a harsh, dry heat which concerned me. *Turbulent* had been alongside in port for a while in this extreme heat, which meant that her systems may be unpredictable. I was right to be worried. The air temperature was 45 degrees which had a severe knock-on effect. As the tugs pulled us out to sea, instead of the excitement I usually felt at this moment, I had a sense of deep foreboding.

In *Novacene*, James Lovelock reminds us that the unconscious mind can identify danger within 40 milliseconds. What's more, in that infinitesimal amount of time, the intuitive part of your brain can come up with a muscular response. That's how we evolved to escape from predators swifter and stronger than us. 'The intuitive mind is a sacred gift', he says, quoting Einstein. 'The rational mind is a faithful servant. We have created a society that honours the servant and has forgotten the gift.'[29] My intuition was telling me something just wasn't right.

We'd got quite a long way from Fujairah; only the mountain tops on the coastline were still visible and I was about to leave the bridge and go below when the Officer of the Watch (OOW) handed me the phone. All the air-conditioning plants had failed. The next three hours were the most challenging of my life.

Descending the ladder to the control room I was immediately hit by a wave of intense heat. It was like a furnace in there, the atmosphere already heavy with tension. We had entered the unknown. Despite all our training and preparation, we were about to be tested to our limits.

The control room lights had all been dimmed and only the equipment vital for life or driving the submarine had been left on. Yet judging by the wave of reports coming through it was clear conditions elsewhere in the submarine were even worse. Back aft, humidity levels had reached 100 per cent. In some areas, the temperature had risen to over 60 degrees. Crew members were overheating. There were signs the situation was escalating out of control.

Heat stress affects everyone differently. It varies depending on your particular physiology, fitness level and even your genetic makeup, to some extent. When you're exposed to extreme heat your body regulates its temperature by evaporating sweat from your skin. But when both air temperature and humidity levels are high, as in this situation, your body's thermo-regulating system is considerably

---

[29] James Lovelock, *Novascene: The Coming of Age of Hyperintelligence*, Penguin, 2019, p.20.

impaired. Your cardiovascular system responds by directing heat to your skin to increase heat transfer which then places considerable strain on your heart. Any physical activity — which of course, we had to do — exacerbates this further.

My medical knowledge was sufficient to know that when your body temperature rises to over 104 degrees Fahrenheit, the risk of heat injury increases dramatically and will impact the function of your central nervous system and organs such as your heart and kidneys. I also knew that regulatory failure can happen quickly in some people and while many sufferers may at first develop mild symptoms, others would become very sick fast. Quite frankly, the prognosis was terrifying.

In a situation like this, any sort of decision-making — let alone sound decision-making — seemed nigh on impossible. Yet I had to make the right call. If I didn't, there was a risk the situation could escalate to a dangerous, if not fatal one, in moments. To cool the submarine we needed to dive, but I'd received reports the foreplanes weren't working and the hatch wasn't sealing properly. Then the first of a succession of reports of casualties came over the main broadcast system.

As temperatures soared and water supplies ran frighteningly low, men everywhere were succumbing to heat exhaustion, displaying symptoms ranging from headaches, dizziness and vomiting to fainting and seizures. I was used to being in charge but this particular battle was relentless. I felt very much alone.

Acknowledging that other people were better equipped to deal with the most critical casualties, I knew I could count on teams and individual crew members to deal with other incidents autonymously too. I had all the puzzle pieces. I just needed to formulate a plan. Fast.

"We'll be all right. I've got a way out of this," I said over and over again as I made my way around the submarine checking my team. Unclothed men lay sweating and panting, propped up against walls or wherever they had dropped. It made negotiating the tight corridors even tricker than usual. In the junior rates' bathroom, the

Petty Officer Medical Assistant (POMA) was spraying people with a hose to keep them cool, reducing water supplies further.

I'd decided returning to Fujairah wasn't an option. *Turbulent* wouldn't make it and neither would the crew. I could ask HQ for help, but it would take longer for them to get helicopters or a frigate out to us than it would take for us to resolve the situation ourselves. Abandonment would undoubtedly result in fatalities, particularly given the external conditions. Waiting for rescue could take hours. If we didn't deal with this effectively, we wouldn't be the only ones impacted; the political consequences for the UK could be catastrophic. Most importantly, however, the risk of losing lives was increasing at a rate of knots.

The heat was affecting me too. Working through the problems one by one took enormous effort but it finally gave me clarity. To cool down the boat, we needed to dive. First I spoke to the team over the main broadcast system.

Having outlined the situation I explained the only solution was to get underwater to cool down. I urged them to look after their shipmates and keep hydrated. To contact HQ would mean switching on the equipment which would intensify the heat and risk writing it off completely. But I needed to alert them to our predicament. After that, to maintain my team's trust in me, I needed to deliver.

In the past, I had led all of them at one time or another — and in some extremely challenging (albeit different) situations too. We had always succeeded. Now was the time to lever off their trust in me.

There were 27 casualties in total and we nearly lost the submarine itself. As we started to lose key players on the team, leadership brought everyone through. We saved the submarine and went back on patrol but in that three-hour period, it took every ounce of my leadership skill to bring us through and enable the team to achieve success.

For me, there are three key elements leaders need in that kind of high-pressure situation:

1. Make sure your team has a shared purpose and vision. You need them to buy into what you're trying to achieve and

enable them to do what they think is right at any time. That's hard work.

2. Make sure that whenever possible, everybody gets a say in the decision-making process, right up to when the decision is made, so that everyone is heading in the same direction. If everyone can have a say, and they know that every intervention is valued, they respond well when things go wrong.

3. Make sure the values of integrity, honesty, shared purpose and so on are continually drilled into people. That way they always know where they fit in.

Pressure points:

- Consistency is key.
- If storytelling isn't your strongest point, develop the skill so you can clearly articulate your vision.
- Learn to lead out of context (it helps tame wicked problems).
- Loyalty is a two-way thing.
- Empower your team but retain the ability to intervene at the right time.

Near miss

HMS *Triumph*. Course 290. Speed 3Kt.
Depth: 45M. Weapon Readiness State 1.
Clyde Exercise Areas. Intelligence gathering. Chartered
Depth: 110M. 1630 ZULU.
Teacher has conduct. You are the Duty Commanding Officer.

"Duty Navigator, SITREP (Situation Report)" you order. The Duty Navigator is another Perisher student, hovering over a WECDIS screen interpreting the information in front of them."

"Duty Captain, we're half a cable to port of our 275 track with a further 1 nautical mile to run to the take position. Sunset is in 15 minutes," he replies.

You acknowledge then pick up the microphone to speak to the Ops team. "Team, we've 1 mile to run. As previously briefed, we'll be returning to periscope depth shortly, get the information and get out. One Merlin is dipping to the north of us, but will find it difficult to detect us and the Type 23 is not held — that doesn't mean she's not out there. Reduced white lighting in the Control Room."

This is always an eerie scene. You've always loved it when the control room goes into red lighting, it reminds you of watching Das Boot and the attacks conducted by the German U-boat team at night. The Control Room team looks ready to go. They're still focused despite the intensity of Perisher and being in the third week.

Teacher is in the Control Room and goes over to the Ship Control Team. "Team, you all well? How's the boat's trim?" you hear him say.

The Ship Control Officer of the Watch, who he's known for a long time, gives him a briefing. Teacher acknowledges and then goes and sits opposite you by the Command Display. He checks his watch and then looks at you.

"AC, let's go," you tell your co-student, and then an evolution full of risk begins as the submarine transitions from depth up to periscope depth.

The risks fall into two categories: safety and counter-detection:

- Safety: because despite the best sonars in the world, if there are boats not putting any sound into the water because they've stopped or are sailing vessels so there's no engine noise, then they could be close and you wouldn't know.
- Counter-detection: because if you don't have control of the submarine once at periscope depth, you could overshoot the right depth and the fin could come out of the water, giving a visual and radar detection opportunity, so you have to get it absolutely right.

The AC looks at Ship Control. "All positions, standby to return to periscope depth," he says loudly. Reports come back telling him that stations within the team are ready. He starts giving propulsion and ship control orders. The submarine angle comes on and the depth reduces.

He's decided to make a tactical return which means keeping the submarine a couple of metres below periscope depth until they prove control, then he'll raise the periscope. They prove control and begin rising the final couple of metres.

After glancing at the sonar screen, Teacher shows you a tiny, faint blip he's noticed. Something's not quite right, you realise. You respond fast.

"AC, investigate bearing 300 immediately," you can feel real tension. The mast goes up. As the periscope gets on the bearing, the AC's eyes widen, betraying visible signs of fear. "Go Deep, Go Deep, Go Deep keep 60 metres, lower Search".

The shock on everyone's face is visible. You have frozen, the Ship Control Team looks at Teacher. "Safeguard – go deep", he shouts. This means it's real.

All hell breaks loose. "Full Ahead, Make the Battleshort, 10 Down Keep 60 metres," the Ship Control Officer of the Watch orders.

"Shut Bulkhead doors," comes over the main broadcast followed by the general alarm.

Teacher is now standing by Ship Control. The AC is sitting on the deck, his face white with shock. The crew is starting to brace for collision. With the planes at full dive the Planesman is calling out the depth: "18 metres, 19 metres, 20 metres."

The captain rushes into the Control Room. It's his boat, his crew. He looks at Ship Control.

"21 metres," the Planesman calls out.

Emergency reports are coming in. The team is responding to the emergency very well. Teacher turns to the AC. "What did you go deep for'?"

"Type 23 frigate. Right ahead, range 500 yards," the AC replies.

"23 metres," the Planesman announces.

Teacher knows the draught of the Type 23, you realise. He takes direct control when *Triumph*'s under it and safe: "Half ahead revolutions 50, keep 30 metres, risk of collision has passed."

Ship Control relays this over the Main Broadcast to the rest of the submarine. The team starts recovering the situation and reverting back to normal.

Teacher walks over to you. You're still in shock.

"This is the true test of your leadership," he says gently, whispering so no one else can hear. " We're all alive. Now compose yourself, gain control and get going fast. The team will forget the moment rapidly." He moves away, looks around the Control Room and after speaking to the Captain turns back to you.

"Duty Captain, are you ready to take back the submarine?" You meet his eye.

"Ready, Sir," you reply, keeping your voice steady.

There is a very brief handover, then looking at the team, you pick up the microphone handset. "Team, this is the Duty Captain. We are safe and in control. We know there is a very quiet Type 23 out there, but it is now being held Sonar track S132. We're in position and we can gather the intelligence. Therefore, standby to return to periscope depth. Let's focus rapidly."

CHAPTER 8

Follow

'He who cannot be a good follower, cannot be a good leader.'

Aristotle.

On 2nd April 2020, Brett E Crozier, Captain of USS Theodore Roosevelt was relieved of duty. An outbreak of coronavirus on board the aircraft carrier prompted him to request help for his virus-stricken crew which numbered over 4,800. Testing revealed over 800 crew members were infected and at least one sailor subsequently died.

Crozier was rebuffed by his superiors for over four days during his efforts to limit the spread of infection. Told to expect over fifty of his crew to die, he sent a letter to three admirals and copied it to seven captains asking for permission to offload all but 10 per cent of the ship's crew. Believing the carrier had insufficient space to isolate or quarantine infected sailors, he pleaded with his superiors for faster intervention. "We are not at war. Sailors do not need to die," Crozier wrote. "If we do not act now, we are failing to properly take care of our most trusted asset — our Sailors".[30] His letter was leaked to the press, creating a political firestorm even Trump got involved with and ended in his dismissal.

Following an investigation, House Armed Services Committee Chairman Adam Smith called on the Defense Secretary to reinstate Crozier. "While Captain Crozier's actions at the outset of the health

---

[30] Brett Crozier quoted in Seapower Magazine, available at: https://seapowermagazine.org/decision-on-croziers-fate-in-the-hands-of-pentagon-officials/ accessed 31 May 2023.

crisis aboard the Theodore Roosevelt were drastic and imperfect, it is clear he only took such steps to protect his crew," Smith said in his statement. "Not only did Captain Crozier have the full support of his crew, he also attempted to work within his chain of command. During this time of crisis, Captain Crozier is exactly what our sailors need: a leader who inspires confidence."[31]

As Crozier departed the ship for the last time, his crew cheered, whistled, clapped and chanted his name.[32] Later, Crozier said he was aware of the impact his decision might have on his career, but his crew's safety was more important. Despite petitions containing over 100,000 signatures, In the summer of 2020, the Navy announced Crozier wouldn't be reinstated.

Early in my command, I did something similar. I brought the submarine back alongside during an extended training period. I'd only been onboard a few weeks, but the crew had been going at this training for a significant period of time and it was obvious to me they were worn out, which meant we weren't progressing as we needed to.

I wrote a message stating my intent: to bring the submarine back alongside and let the crew take a break, fill in some gaps with simulator training, regroup and go again after Christmas. This was not well received and it resulted in some quite heated discussions with one of my superiors, the Senior Leader in Tactical Command.

I stood my ground, asked him to judge me on the decision, manage the HQ's expectations and explain why I'd made the decision, even if it wasn't what he would do. I didn't share the content of the conversation I'd had with my superior with the crew, but the crew saw that I genuinely cared. But that was not the only benefit of bringing the submarine back alongside. The break rejuvenated the crew, they were able to prepare again and we were certified for operations — a successful outcome which in turn, benefited my superiors.

---

[31] Adam Smith quoted in The Hill, available at: https://thehill.com/policy/defense/navy/494553 accessed 31 May 2023.
[32] CBS News, 9 January 2020.

What I learned from this experience was when to lead, when to be a consigliere and when and how to follow. I also learned that you don't share criticism of HQ with anyone, which can be difficult.

When to lead, when to act as consigliere and when to follow

Few people understand that leadership is also about followership — you lead people and you are led, whatever your position. Even a CEO answers to a Board or shareholders. Over time, the number of people you follow will decrease but to be a successful leader, you need both skill sets.

A leader who only leads believes they have no room for improvement. This is short-sighted. Leadership is an ongoing journey, one in which you need the opportunity for personal growth and development as much as your team. Reject the idea of followership and you're sentencing yourself to remaining stuck at your current level of personal development.

However, followership is a complex art, particularly when you're a leader. There will be times when you must step up to the plate, take charge and make decisions in the team's best interests, occasions when it's more appropriate to be a consigliere or adviser, and situations where you should step back and let someone else lead. You need to be able to recognise these and act accordingly and that requires self-awareness and an understanding of your strengths and weaknesses. You should also be able to read a situation and the people involved, determine the best course of action and then communicate it effectively.

Let's take these three types of leadership roles one by one:

Leader

Leading is required when there's a crisis when major change is needed or when there's a lack of direction or clarity. In each situation, you must be able to take control and guide the team through it.

1. Crisis situations

A crisis could come in the form of a natural disaster, financial collapse or a security breach. Whatever the crisis is, you'll need to make quick decisions to protect your team (as well as the company and its stakeholders). That might mean making difficult decisions about budget cuts, redundancies or restructuring.

2. High-stakes decisions

Entering a new market, launching a new product or acquiring another company are all occasions requiring a major decision to be made, one that could have a significant impact on the organisation. You'll need to take charge. Weigh the potential risks and make a decision that's in your team's best interests.

3. Lack of direction

When there's a lack of direction or clarity within the team, it's your role to set the vision, articulate it clearly, communicate expectations and create a plan to achieve the goals.

4. Change

Stepping up often means tackling something no one else is willing to do. Sometimes that's acknowledging that something needs to be done differently. As a leader, it's down to you to officially recognise things aren't working and need to change.

Paradoxically, stepping up can also mean stepping back and empowering others in your team to shine. It's a way to underline to your team that you're all in the same boat together. A step up, step back approach means you'll do more than usual in the early stages of change, then step back and do less. Effective leaders understand that stepping back isn't the same as delegating. That's a top-down approach that can stifle and demotivate.

Stepping back is different. It's about leading from the ground up. You set your team up for success by encouraging and developing their skills, so they grow beyond what they thought they were capable of. You also create a culture in which failure is seen as part of the process.

Consigliere

Consiglieri effectively lead from the shadows. They are, if you like, the thinking partners in decision-making. Although the word is associated with the Mafia — immediately bringing to mind movies like *The Godfather* — some of the greatest leaders in history enjoyed the support and partnership of a trusted adviser who promoted their vision and, in many cases, helped them rise to power. Aristotle himself acted as consigliere to Alexander the Great, shaping his thinking on everything from leadership and race to maths and philosophy. (The Macedonian King is said to have developed a passion for the works of Homer as a result).

In business terms, acting as consigliere is about providing guidance, counsel, support and expertise to other decision-makers within your organisation (including your superiors). Depending on your area of expertise that might mean offering insight into a business strategy, assisting with complex negotiations or advising on regulatory requirements.

You may need to act as a consigliere during a potential merger or acquisition, for example, advising on market trends and risks. Or you might recommend negotiating strategies when brokering a deal. Just remember your role is to listen carefully and provide support and advice without overstepping the boundaries. That includes taking over the situation or making decisions on a superior's behalf.

Follower

Followership is rarely taught and yet it's expected without hesitation. But just as there's an art to leadership, there's an art to followership too. Followership is not about blindly following where a leader has decided to go or accepting decisions without question, it's about contributing to the *team* to the maximum of your ability.

There are three elements to followership:

1. Adding value

Followers add value to the team. In a submarine, this initial value comes from wearing a submarine badge. If you wear the badge, you are qualified. So while you may not be an expert in a particular field, if something goes wrong you'll be able to deal with it confidently until specialists can take over. The same is true in business.

You also add value by contributing to the final outcome. Specialist, general and personal capabilities are important to achieving success as a team. A key part of followership is ensuring that you offer up everything you have, accepting that even if it's not used on that occasion, you will continue to do so.

2. Challenge

Most teams have a 'red cell' — personnel who can think out of the box. The best-operated submarines choose people who can think like that to overcome group thinking. This is particularly useful in the planning stages when you're trying to think as the enemy might and prepare accordingly.

This is only one form of challenge, however. Followership also entails challenging a leader's decisions before they make them. But this *must* be constructive. In some organisations, you may find there are boundaries and hierarchies to consider. You may also find that those in leadership roles will have different tolerance levels when it comes to being challenged. Moreover, not all followers will want to challenge. It's therefore important to establish a symbiotic relationship between follower and leader.

As I said in Chapter 5, during my command of *Turbulent*, I made it clear that we were a democracy right up until I made the decision. From then on, we went forward together as one. However, I also encouraged my HODs to challenge me afterwards (albeit subtly).

I needed this in order to continuously evaluate my decision. It became an integral part of our team psyche because change never fails when it's affected early with a plan and reason. It fails when it's done late with no plan.

In the business world, I've seen this done well; I've also seen it done badly. In 2019, I was brought into CityFibre as a director to lead a team delivering full fibre networks nationwide. I was excited by this opportunity. I bought into the CEO's vision at my interview. He was a charismatic individual, able to use warfare language — I really wanted to work for that company, I thought. But when I actually started work for the organisation it wasn't what it had seemed.

There was a small group of people who'd been with the CityFibre from the outset who basically, would never let anyone else in. The firm brought in several experienced leaders like me, but none of us were ever admitted into the 'huddle'. This becomes disruptive. You'll make a decision, only to find it's been undone by somebody else with influence above you. And because you're excluded from this niche group, you don't feel part of the team, which creates a really unhappy working environment.

By contrast, at First Light Fusion, everybody is included in decisions — everyone has a voice. It doesn't mean they get to make the decision but everyone is consulted. Instead of saying, "I think the decision is [whatever it is] but we need to consult", we take a different approach. We start by saying "What is the problem we're trying to solve?" and then consult within an agreed timeframe. (Without a timeframe, there's a danger, more and more information is brought into the process which may or may not be useful.) Once the decision has been made we then explain why we made it. Fusion is a brilliant example of the benefits of a symbiotic relationship between leaders and followers.

3. Support

Out of the three elements of followership, support is the most vital. Even if you're initially unable to add value, or challenge effectively (especially if you've just joined an organisation) you must support constructively. This may be in the form of research, informed opinion or sacrifice- but it must ensure the outcome.

Support could be in the form of your acquiescence to a decision or a particular course of action. It may sometimes be relatively simple to achieve — it's clear and straightforward. On other occasions, it may challenge your morals and ethics.

Work out where your boundaries are, where you're willing to support and where it will be difficult, if not impossible. If it *is* going to be difficult make sure you've carefully thought through how you are going to communicate or challenge effectively.

How to be critical without undermining leadership

As I mentioned at the beginning of this chapter, I learned early on in my command not to share criticism of HQ with others. As a result, in my *Perisher Guide to Taking Command,* I gave the following advice to student captains:

> *Your loyalty to your submarine should never be in conflict with your loyalty to your Flotilla and higher command. COs who forget this allow a rivalry to develop which ends up isolating their submarine, making relationships and interaction with the Flotilla difficult. This, in turn, can lead to resentment. Overt criticism of higher command within your submarine may create short-term unity but in the long term, it's damaging and breeds cynicism.*

> *Reputations are quickly earned this way and rarely shaken off. The most successful submarines are in harmony with higher command; the best COs those who cultivate a relationship of mutual trust and confidence and readily seek their superiors' advice. Without this attitude, there will be limited Flotilla team spirit and the efficiency of your submarine will undoubtedly suffer.*

This advice is equally relevant to business leaders. As I said in the previous chapter, loyalty is a two-way thing and that includes your loyalty to those above you (even though they may be few, depending on where you are in your leadership journey). Your loyalty to your team should work in unison with your loyalty to your Chairman, CEO and/or stakeholders. Sharing criticism of your superiors with your team can be divisive, impact morale, affect engagement and ultimately, corrode team spirit.

However, constructive feedback is invaluable for everyone in the workplace — leaders included — for several reasons.

- It helps identify blind spots — when you're busy and juggling a host of different responsibilities, you may be blinkered to areas you need to improve upon
- It encourages growth and development — developing new skills to improve areas where you may be weak will make you more effective in your role.
- It builds trust and respect between leader and team, creating a positive and productive work environment.
- It promotes open and honest communication between leader and team building trust and loyalty.

But being critical can be difficult, especially when it involves providing feedback to someone in a position of authority. So how do you go about it without undermining their leadership?

First, focus on behaviours not character or personality. This avoids feedback sounding more like a personal attack. Keep the conversation focused on the issue at hand. For example, instead of saying "You're too cold when giving direction," say "Your communication could be improved when delegating tasks".

Second, acknowledge the positive aspects of their leadership before discussing the negative and watch your tone. To keep the conversation productive you want to sound supportive without coming across as patronising.

Use specific examples to illustrate your points and if necessary, provide additional context. If your criticism is about communication, explain when this occurred and how it impacted the team. It may also be helpful to offer potential solutions, too. It shows you're invested in the team's success as a whole.

Pressure points:

- Leadership is also about followership; you need both skill sets to be a good leader.
- Followership is an art, particularly for leaders.
- Know when to lead, when to be consiglieri and how to follow.
- Learn how to be critical without undermining leadership.

Safe water

HMS *Triumph*. Course 290. Speed 3Kt. Depth: 45M.
Weapon Readiness State 1.
Clyde Exercise Areas. Intelligence gathering. Chartered
Depth: 110M. 1630 ZULU.
Teacher has conduct. The Duty Commanding Officer is
Lt Cdr Jensen.
You are the AC.

You are standing next to the Duty Captain who is sitting in the Captain's chair, his eyes fixed on the command console. He looks concerned — and rightly so. This tactical situation is not good and levered against you. There's a serious amount of 'opposition' out there: 2 frigates, 3 helicopters and more coming...

You know the Duty Captain knows this. And because you've been the Duty Captain, you know what he's going through. You also know that if you're successful and you pass Perisher, you'll become an XO and you'll do this for real, with real effect.

You go over to the WECDIS screen to speak to the Duty Navigator. "How much safe water have we got?" you ask quietly.

'Safe water' is a term used by submariners to define in three dimensions the amount of water in which the submarine has to manoeuvre. It restricts where you operate and how you operate. At some points, you can only operate at periscope depth which can be really constraining because you're limited by the amount of speed you can use.

You quickly assess the information the Duty Navigator gives you and head back to the periscope.

"All positions, AC. Standby All Round Look', you announce, kneeling down to meet the periscope eyepieces as the mast comes up.

"Raise search," you say, starting your stopwatch and seeing the periscope raise under hydraulic pressure.

You know what you're expecting to see from the sonar picture, but there are always surprises so you must really concentrate only on what you can see through the periscope because you'll need to relay that back to the team.

"Breaking clear," you say as the mast clears the water line. In the next 30 seconds, as you rotate the mast, you must take in everything you see. You clock the masts of a warship over the horizon. "Mark that bearing. Warship, Type 23, 10000 yards, 30 starboard", you call out while continuing the ARL.

As you reach the end of the 360 look, you announce "lower search," stepping away from the periscope as it lowers and then brief the team on what you have seen.

'AC, Duty Captain. What's your look interval?"

You give him a time, and he acknowledges. "Duty Captain, can you come over to WECDIS?"

As you both head over, to the WECDIS you want to give him your assessment of the situation and your opinion about changing the plan. You know you only have two minutes to do this before you need to do another ARL.

"Sir, I know this is the current plan," you begin, keeping your voice measured and calm, "but I believe that the situation has changed. The Modus Operandi of the Type 23 doesn't fit the profile we expect."

"Why do you say that? I think this is similar to what I expected" he replies. You start sharing your reasoning and then have to break away to prepare for the next ARL.

After another ARL, you come back to the Duty Captain and quietly discuss your reasoning in more detail. You think he should consider changing the plan, you tell him. He disagrees. You have a different experience set and viewpoint to him, but he's made his decision so you go back to managing the surface picture.

Over the next 12 minutes, you still observe behaviour which doesn't match what you'd expect. Yet no one else is calling it out. Out of earshot of others, you mention your concerns again to the Duty Captain. He's still convinced his plan is the right one so again you acknowledge and carry on with supporting the mission.

"Ops Controller'." says the Sonar Controller. "Target zig on Track 204 classified Type 23 – aspect change and increase in speed – TPK indicates 25 knots."

"Transmissions Watcher, Bearing 090 classified 2050 fitted to Track 204."

The situation you predicted has materialised. There is less safe water, no time and action needs to be taken. You could give into frustration but what's the point? It won't change the situation. Being a follower means challenging constructively, and you've done that. All you can do now is help the Duty Captain.

"AC, how do you assess the situation?" he now asks. He's not asking for ideas, but he does need the right factual information and, potentially, your analysis which you must give in a constructive way. You start to share your assessment making sure you clarify what is fact and what is your analysis. He listens, you watch him absorb the information, then he briefs the team. He changes the plan and begins evasion.

CHAPTER 9

The Prize

Rear Admiral Cain: "The end is inevitable, Maverick.
Your kind is headed for extinction."

Captain Pete 'Maverick' Mitchell: "Maybe so, sir. But not today."

Top Gun: Maverick.

Taking command is a privilege, it is not a right — so is leading. The prize (if you really need one) is legacy. You should want to be remembered for having done the right thing and for serving your crew.

Some potential submarine captains believe that because they've passed Perisher, they should automatically be given respect and can step in anywhere and command. You can step into the role, but if you think there is no need to earn respect and it's all about 'your moment', you'll get it very wrong. It's not about you and what you will do now you've qualified, it's about how you enable the next generation. Their success is your gift and legacy. You must take people's development seriously and *be seen* to take it seriously too.

Not long after I left the military, I attended my class reunion at the Royal Naval College in Dartmouth. It had been twenty-five years since I'd joined up. Going back into that environment felt a bit surreal although in some respects it felt as if I'd never been away. I found myself reflecting on my crew. This wasn't unusual, even now I'll seize every opportunity I get to reminisce with others in the submarine service. We all seem to spend a lot of time talking about the great times we had as a team. It's a bit like having a support group called Turbulent Anonymous! It still feels good to know I was able to contribute and that for those just starting out on their leadership journey, I set a good example. All the crew were such individuals (even the challenging ones!) and made our journey together so incredible. I hope I gave everyone the chance to explore their real abilities and perhaps that contributed to our success.

During the reunion, a young midshipman approached me.

"Sir,—" he said as he stepped forward.

"I've left the navy," I smiled and put out my hand to shake his. "You don't need to call me sir. Please call me Ryan."

'You won't remember me, but I visited the simulator when you were teaching Perisher last year. You trained me and one of my fellow midshipmen to conduct a visual attack. Afterwards, you told us that the whole thing about leadership was serving your team and that submarines were the best place to do that. You also told us that we should never worry about what the issue is; it's how you deal with it that counts. We did that, and we've passed."

The ultimate prize — influence the next generation positively. I enjoyed that feeling.

Stepping into someone else's shoes

Taking over command of a submarine can sometimes be a challenging process.

I knew I'd been selected to command *Turbulent* 18 months before I joined the submarine and during the lead-up, I spent a lot of time thinking about how I was going to make a positive effect. The culmination of my training and ambition, after 20 years in the Navy, it was my first command.

I visualised myself in the new role, planned for it and read any information I could lay my hands on about how others had done it before me. Being mentally as well as physically prepared for it was incredibly important to me. Until then, there had always been someone I could turn to. Even as an XO or second in command,

I could defer to my captain. Once I took command 130 people's lives were my responsibility and mine alone.

In November 2008, I received an unexpected call from my future boss.

"Ryan, it's Captain SM," he said. "We've had a discussion and the decision has been made for you to take command on Monday. We know that as the crew is mid-training this is unusual, but now's the time. Are you happy with that?"

The sudden change in plan took me by surprise but I replied without missing a beat. "Yes, sir, absolutely. I'll liaise with the travel people and get it sorted."

In Chapter 3, I explained the challenges of taking over a well-established team mid-way through training but I was also taking over from an extremely popular captain.

There's a routine procedure when a navy vessel changes hands which typically takes around twenty minutes. I had a fairly good idea of what to expect after a chat with a frigate captain who'd recently taken over as 'driver' of an aircraft carrier.

"It can be a bit of an emotional roller coaster," he said. "It doesn't take long but it's best to prepare yourself. Once you've taken command, your predecessor leaves and the crew cheer him over the gangway. The size of the cheer indicates the popularity of the previous captain, and that can be a bit daunting."

It was late afternoon when I arrived in Faslane. Rain had fallen and the ground was still wet. Ominous-looking dark clouds hung low still in the sky, providing a dramatic backdrop for my first glimpse of *Turbulent*. *There she is,* I thought as I caught sight of her. She looked incredible. I was itching to get on board but protocols had to be observed.

All ships and submarines follow the same protocol: a new captain does not go aboard until he takes command. But it appeared my predecessor was in no rush to hand over. (Later, when it came to my turn to hand over *Turbulent*, I could sympathise. It's an emotionally-charged moment.) Curbing my anticipation, I remained in my cabin ashore preparing my kit and reflecting on the words of wisdom provided by others.

"Ryan, remember two things," my friend Mike Bernacchi, captain of the USS *Alexandria* had advised. "Firstly, don't change who you are, but be aware of yourself. Secondly, you are not their friend, their brother or their father — you're their captain, which is all of those and none."

On my arrival at *Turbs* the next morning at 08.45, XO Dan Clarke, the second in command, was there to greet me with a salute as I headed over the gangway. After a polite briefing where he explained what would happen next during the formal process of taking command, I was at last shown into the captain's cabin.

The only single cabin on board, the captain's cabin is tiny. It's not much bigger than your average downstairs toilet at home. It's located next to the control room and the reactor compartment opposite the radio room and you'll find it in much the same place on attack submarines everywhere in the world. It means the captain can get to the control room instantly. Because when things go wrong on a submarine they usually go wrong very fast.

"Welcome, Ryan," said the captain, shaking my hand. He was friendly enough but I sensed instantly that this was not a good day for him. He looked like a man not ready to give up command and seeing my eagerness to take over probably didn't help.

"Hello, mate," I replied, smiling, doing my best to sound friendly and relaxed. "How do we take this from here?"

He looked hard at me for a few seconds as if weighing me up, then nodded. "The submarine is in a good material state and the HODs will brief you," he said, his voice flat. There was an awkward silence, and then he turned and picked up some papers from the desk behind him.

"Here are the combinations to the safes," he said, briskly — as if he'd suddenly decided to get this part over with as quickly as possible.

"Which one is which?" I asked, keeping my tone light, still trying to sound friendly.

Another silence. I could see he was struggling to maintain his composure. To ease his discomfort, I pretended not to notice, but there and then I decided that when my turn came to relinquish command of the submarine, I would do it differently. There had to be another way.

The conversation continued in the same, stilted vein until mercifully Dan, the XO, appeared saying it was time to leave.

The captain shook my hand once more. "Good luck," he said, his voice muted before he turned and followed Dan from the cabin.

I stood there alone for some minutes, holding my breath, listening. Then it came — an enormous cheer. That was quite a send-off, I thought, realising I had a huge task ahead of me. The outgoing captain may not have been very welcoming to me but he was clearly a huge hit with the crew. I may have a long way to go before I really became their leader.

Any leader stepping into someone else's shoes is faced with the challenge of dealing with their predecessor's accomplishments and shortcomings. You might know how the team's been led before, you might not. You could be taking over from someone brilliant, who's led so well, the team mourns their departure. Or from someone they're glad to see the back of. None of this matters. Neither does the 'why': people get promoted, people move on and people get moved on. It's all part of life.

However, taking over from someone who was well-liked requires a different approach to taking over from someone who battered the team. Let's take a look at each of these situations in turn.

Taking over from someone who was well-liked

I've always thought taking over from someone popular is easier than taking over from a poor leader. After all, your predecessor has done everything for you already; you're inheriting a great team and system. If you remove your ego from the equation, this is easy. The focus must be on the relationship between you and your team. And a great team just wants the same — continuing good leadership.

The reality, of course, is that you may or may not match their needs but as long as the team stays stable, you're good. They'll adapt; you'll adapt. Having taken over from a good leader on several occasions, I've learned the most important thing is communicating the 'what' and the 'why' and assuring people they still have the 'how'. Here are a few pointers that may help you in a similar situation:

1. Take your ego out of the equation
Stop worrying whether you'll be better than the person you're taking over from. It's not a competition. You're there to serve the team as a leader.

2. Get to know your people fast
Walk the teak. Get to know each team member individually — face to face, not virtually.

3. Adapt to your team, not the other way around
Adapt your leadership style to your team. Don't make them adapt to you. It's easier for one person to make some adjustments than it is for 150 to 200 people to change.

4. Start with simple changes
If you want to make some changes, start with the simple stuff — the quick wins.

5. Choose your words
If there's best practice you can bring in from other organisations then great. But be careful how you describe it to your team. I learned this the hard way on the oil rig.

To begin with, I'd preface every sentence with "In the submarine service, we…" or, "This worked great in the submarine service". Don't do this. It makes people think what they're doing in this organisation isn't up to scratch. And that's not good for morale. Find a more subtle way to introduce a new practice. Tell them the why (the time-saving, for example) then suggest 'we' give it a go.

Taking over from a poor or controversial leader

To my mind, taking over from a poor leader is a greater challenge. You'll wonder why they were ever in a position to lead and influence people but there's no point dwelling on it. You've just got to get on and work out how to sort the mess they've left behind.

I've gained real satisfaction from turning these situations around and showing people what good leadership can do. However, I've never enjoyed the start of the process. This is because I can't solve the 'why?':

- Why do people lead like this?
- Why do people allow others to lead them like this?

When you're taking over from a poor, or controversial leader, you may find you have to be accountable for their mistakes. At the same time, you must create a new vision for the team. On top of that, poor leadership takes its toll on an organisation and that can mean you need to take dynamic action to remedy its impact. Even for the most seasoned of leaders, this can be a difficult balance to manage.

But you do have to take action and be seen to be doing so. Fast. Your team may be expecting nothing to change — particularly if they don't know you. They need to see something different — so show them. Make small changes early on that have a positive impact. By preparing before taking over and validating the plan on arrival you'll be able to *do* and be *seen to be doing*.

When I've been in this situation in the past, I've used the same strategy and tactics because they work for me. Most of these skills have already been shared with you in this book. There's just one thing to add — and it's crucial. When you're taking over from a poor or controversial leader, you must avoid criticising them to your team.

Avoid criticising poor leadership

I'm not suggesting you ignore your forerunner's failings or mistakes, especially if they were unpopular or controversial. Nor should you blame them for all the problems currently facing your team. Instead, you should acknowledge the past, which also means acknowledging the good that particular leader did. Because no matter how poor their leadership was, it's more than likely they had good points too. For example, Commander X, the captain who had the most impact on me and taught me how *not* to lead, was very effective at dealing with outside authorities when readying the submarine for operations.

As you get round your team and they become comfortable with you, they'll probably share their experiences of their previous leader with you. When that happens, you have a choice. You can either choose to move the conversation gently on, or allow them to share.

If you choose to let them share, listen — listen to their concerns but avoid commenting on your predecessor. In this situation, I always let someone vent — they often need to — but I never say, "Yeah, I agree, that's really poor leadership".

You should also discuss any trauma and damage your predecessor may have caused (again, without criticising them). You'll fail if you see yourself solely as the force of restoration without taking the time to understand the full impact on the team. Ask individuals and your team as a whole open-ended questions, like "What do you need going forward?" "How can I enable this?" "What are you hoping I will/won't do?" Their answers will help you determine what the organisation needs to recover and evolve. You can then use this information to inform your vision. And while you may find you're having lots of these kinds of conversations at the outset, they'll gradually decrease as life improves.

You'll probably need to vent to someone yourself. In this situation, I discuss things with my mentor. We agree never to talk about the individual concerned, however. Instead we discuss behaviours, their impact on the team and recovery options.

How to change the culture subtly to deliver results

I'm often asked how you go about changing a company culture when you step into a new leadership role. The answer is, subtly. And don't try to change everything at once. I usually look for tweaks I can make here and there to improve the culture and get the results we're looking for.

You could start small with process. How are meetings run? Could that process be altered to give time back to the teams and increase productivity? What about one-to-ones? How often do they happen? How long do they take? (As long as they need to, I would hope.)

It amazes me how many organisations don't have one-to-one sessions. When I'm coaching, I'll ask, "How do you feel that you haven't been given a one-to-one this week?"

The answer, invariably, is "They're busy. So apparently I'm less important than whatever else they're doing." The next point they'll typically make is about feedback. "Without a regular one-to-one, how can they expect me to know whether I'm doing what Im meant to be doing?"

It's vital that individuals feel heard and can get feedback if it's important to them. Introducing one-to-ones and making sure managers actually do them is a quick win when it comes to changing company culture.

Changing work patterns is a slightly bigger tweak. But adapting working hours from a rigid nine to five to something more flexible can be a quick way to change the atmosphere. "I don't expect you to be here nine to five, but I do expect outcomes," you could say. " Then lead by example.

Again, it always comes down to having conversations with people. The more you get to know them, the more you build trust. They see some good wins, they feel the working environment is happier and that has a knock-on effect on the team dynamic.

I've already talked about how we introduced the T-shirts on the oil rig and its effect on the team dynamic. There was also Christmas. I didn't tell them this was what we did in the Navy (I'd learned from my earlier mistake) but at Christmas, the Captain and Officers always served the crew their turkey with all the trimmings. When I was offshore for Christmas, that's exactly what we did. The leadership team served them their Christmas dinner. It was just a small, subtle change but the effect was amazing.

Here are a few more tips:

- Find advocates — they'll do much of this for you.
- Invite everyone to have a say in the debate about what sort of company culture they want. Remind them. "We're a democracy. When the decision is made we move together."
- Don't underestimate the power of branded kit. It creates a feeling of cohesion in the team.
- Celebrate successes, however small.
- Capture the changes: conduct surveys if you like or just walk the teak and find out what your team thinks.

How to manage your emotions

"When we see a stroke aimed and just ready to fall upon the leg or arm of another person, we naturally shrink and draw back our own leg or our own arm;" wrote the philosopher Adam Smith in 1759.[33] This imitation of what was happening to someone else was almost a reflex, he decided and described it as sympathy (although nowadays we'd probably call it empathy). Centuries later, brain imaging studies reveal he was right. The same brain structures activated when we feel our own emotions are also activated when we see these emotions in

---

[33] Adam Smith, *The Theory of Moral Sentiments*, Millar, 1759, p.4.

someone else.[34] Effectively, we're hard-wired to feel what other people feel which can lead to the spread of emotion from person to person or even sweep an entire company. It's a recognised phenomenon that psychologists researching the science of emotion called 'emotional contagion'.

Humans are natural mimics. Our survival depended on our ability to connect with others and mirroring emotion was a way to do that. But studies show that this mirroring happens in milliseconds because it's a subconscious reaction rather than a conscious one. When emotional contagion spreads happiness and positivity, that's a good thing. But of course, negativity is just as easily spread. And while negative emotions such as anxiety can be helpful in moderation, in business, letting your emotions get the better of you can lead to poor decision-making.

According to the theoretical physicist, Leonard Mlodinow, "Studies of emotional intelligence show that the most successful business, political, and religious leaders are usually the ones who can control their emotions and use them as tools when they interact with others. While IQ scores may correlate to cognitive abilities, control over and knowledge of one's emotional state is what is most important for professional and personal success."[35]

What's more, being able to regulate your emotions, enhances your physical wellbeing. Scientists aren't quite certain why, exactly, but they suspect it's because your body's stress response system is activated less frequently.

So how do you deal with your own emotions?

1. Develop stoicism

Although stoic philosophy has been around for over 2,000 years, there's recently been a resurgence of interest in it. However, stoicism

---

[34] Frederique de Vignemont & Tania Singer, 'The Empathic Brain: How, When, and Why?', *Trends in Cognitive Sciences* 10, 2006, pp.435-41.
[35] Leonard Mlodinow, *Emotional: The New Thinking About Feelings*, Penguin, 2022, p.187.

is often misunderstood. It's not about avoiding your emotions, it's about not allowing yourself to be manipulated by them. It's about working on those things you *can* control, not wasting mental energy on the things you can't. For me, Marcus Aurelius, one of the most famous of the Stoic philosophers and ruler of the Roman Empire for almost two decades, defines it best. In his book of essays, *Meditations*, he explains that when you're upset by external events what you're *really* upset about is how you think about those events, not the events themselves.[36]

Suppose you've just lost a major client and your team is feeling demotivated and uncertain about the future. As a leader, it's natural to feel stressed or anxious about the situation. But instead of letting your emotions spin out of control, use stoicism to manage them and make rational decisions in the face of this uncertainty.

- Remind yourself setbacks like this are natural in business but are also opportunities to learn and grow.
- Instead of dwelling on what went wrong, focus on identifying solutions and taking action to move forward.
- Next, adopt a long-term perspective. Business success is never a straight line, there are ups and downs along the way.
- Stay focused on the bigger picture and avoid becoming bogged down in the short-term challenges. Remind yourself and your team of your vision for the company and the progress you've already made towards achieving your goals.

Adopting a stoic approach means you train yourself to focus only on what you can do in a situation to respond positively. Effectively, you're using your emotion to motivate rather than sabotage yourself.

---

[36] Marcus Aurelius and Gregory Hays, *Meditations: A New Translation*, Random House, 2002.

2. Reappraise the situation

Appraisal is what psychologists call the process your brain goes through when making sense of something that just happened. Some of this happens unconsciously, but as it also takes place on a conscious level, you do have some control over it. Studies show you can choose the meaning you assign to an event or circumstance through reappraisal. Effectively, you train yourself to put a different spin on things. When you do this you're short-circuiting the cycle that may otherwise lead to an unwanted emotion.

Let's say one of your team members resigned unexpectedly and at a critical time. This person was an important contributor to the team and now there's a gap in the team's capabilities. It's natural to feel frustrated, disappointed and perhaps a little overwhelmed by the situation. However, you can, if you choose, reappraise it and find an alternative perspective.

- Remind yourself your team member may have had their own reasons for leaving. It's most likely not personal, nor a reflection of your leadership or the team's performance.
- Next, instead of dwelling on the loss, focus on the opportunity it presents to reassess the team's strengths and weaknesses and identify areas for improvement.
- Finally, adopt a growth mindset. Setbacks are inevitable, the most important thing is to keep moving forward. Commit to learning from the situation, identifying solutions and taking action to improve your team's performance and achieve its goals.

3. Express yourself in writing

Expressing an unwanted emotion can help diffuse it. Research reveals that the act of writing down your emotion about an event changes the way you feel about it.[37] Simply expressing your feelings in

---

[37] Mathew, D. Lieberman et al., 'Putting feelings into words', *Psychological Science* 18, 2007, pp. 421-428.

an email and saving it in your drafts folder without sending it, often causes those emotions to subside leaving you better able to handle the situation and act appropriately. (Although rather than risk hitting the send button by mistake, journaling may be a safer option.)

How do you determine what 'good' looks like?

Good leaders are a special breed, and they are rare. Junior leaders regularly tell me how poor some of the leadership is that they experience and how frustrating it is when they want to improve, but have no example to follow. I believe this is because many organisations nowadays are run by managers who are not particularly good leaders.

There's a growing body of evidence to support this. Gallup, for example, has found that companies fail to choose the right candidate with the right talent for the job 82 per cent of the time. As a result, in 2012, only 13 per cent of employees were engaged at work worldwide, a figure which has remained pretty consistent over the past decade. To make matters worse, bad managers cost businesses billions each year — having too many of them can even bring down a company.[38]

If you open your thesaurus, you'll probably find it says the best synonym for *leadership* is *management*. I disagree. As I said in Chapter 7, management is a science; leadership is an art and there's a fundamental difference between the two: managers have employees; leaders have followers. As a follower, both in the submarine service and in the corporate world, I've learned to identify good leaders — those I'll willingly follow into battle (literally and figuratively) because they inspire, motivate and encourage the team to achieve its full potential. I've also learned to spot the bad ones. Those whose poor leadership results in a disengaged workforce, average performance and a high attrition rate.

Many people think leadership is simply about being in charge, having all the answers and being the most qualified or intelligent

---

[38] Jim Harter, Gallup Business Journal, 2023.

person in the room. That's not the case at all. Leadership is about effectively communicating a vision, inspiring people to help achieve it, and empowering others to reach their potential. So how do you determine what 'good' looks like?

To my mind, the real test of leadership is whether you can identify the qualities that make you a good leader and pass these on to others, developing them as leaders themselves. So, what are those qualities? I've touched on many of these in this book and while some of these, such as communication, are skills you can learn and hone over time, the most important leadership qualities are to do with your core values and mindset.

As I said in Chapter 2, you cannot lead if you don't know yourself. Leading without self-knowledge harms your team. A good leader knows who they are, where they're heading and what their values are. Most importantly, they live by these values — leading by example.

Theirs is a growth mindset. This means instead of asking what they can get out of a situation for themselves, they'll ask how they can add value or contribute for others. They're consistent, positive (even if they're not feeling it) take pleasure in enabling others to develop and actively encourage collaboration and creativity.

A leader can only lead if they have followers. Good leaders inspire followership because they take the trouble to really know their people and, because they understand that people are inspired by the way they're made to feel, they are quick to read situations and manage their own emotions.

They are present, self-aware (even in high-pressure situations) and sensitive to the way their behaviour can impact and influence the team.

A poor leader, on the other hand, has little self-awareness and no sense of where they're going. They take from people rather than empower or give because they have a competitive rather than collaborative mindset. Any success is theirs, not the team's. A refusal to be accountable for their mistakes means failure is always someone else's fault and while they demand loyalty they're typically reluctant to bestow the recognition the team's hard work deserves.

In the absence of a good role model, I hope this book will help junior leaders on their journey. For those of you who are already well on your way, I hope you've gleaned some useful insights. Wherever you are on your leadership path, keep learning, stay humble and never, ever, make it about you.

I'll leave you with the rules that shaped my leadership.

My personal, pressure points:

- Serve your team — both leaders and followers
- Know the enemy — it's not always obvious
- Know the context — it drives how you operate
- Plan, understand risk, decide
- Always have an exit
- Celebrate success — theirs.

Congratulations, Captain

HMS *Triumph*. Course 180 Speed 6Kt.
Depth:17.5 metres, Weapon Readiness State 1.
Clyde Exercise Areas, Mini War 2, Chartered Depth: 110M.
1130 ZULU.
Captain has conduct. You are the Duty Commanding Officer.

The Control Room is really busy. It's rammed with extra people today. In addition to the crew, students and Teacher there are lots of VIPs here to witness the final Perisher weekend: a Royal Marine Brigadier; two Rear Admirals; Captain Training North; a couple of senior Police officers; and some civilian guests. The civilians are there to see what the submarine is capable of as well as how the Perisher students are assessed.

Before embarking the guests, Teacher made it clear to the students and crew how this was going to work.

"If everyone starts concentrating on the VIPs we will make mistakes, so you have permission to concentrate on your job. The Captain and I have agreed that I will have 'conduct' and will concentrate on keeping the submarine safe while assessing the students. Some of the guests will not know how important what you do is in any position, how could they? If they ask questions that might distract you, just politely state you need to concentrate, and that you'll answer later if that's okay. I will brief them when they arrive, so they understand too. Any questions Men?" Teacher says to a packed Senior Rates mess.

Was that only two days ago? It feels a lot longer. A week ago, two of the students failed the course. They'd got so far but Teacher had decided they were not going to command. They left the submarine almost immediately by helicopter.

When you went up to say goodbye before you took charge of the helicopter transfer, both students were in the Captain's cabin dressed in immersion suits ready for the transfer, each holding their bag and a bottle of Bells. The whisky is traditionally given — a consolation prize meant to dampen the pain of failure.

"I'm gutted, but it is what it is mate. We tried, we failed. Teacher's told us why and we'll be looked after when we get shore side. Good luck mate, and we'll get in touch when it's all over" says one.

'I don't even like whisky!' says the other, raising his bottle. You all smile. Even though this is a submarine career-limiting event and will take time for both men to get over, humour is still important.

Now, on the last day of the course, what with the intensity of operations and opposition, the pressure has been fierce. Under serious stress, some of your decisions haven't been the best.

Teacher stopped giving feedback and advice a while ago. Instead, he's been asking lots of questions and just watching. He stood at the back of the Control Room talking to the Navigator running the Navigation Safety Cell while they conduct this operation. One of the Admirals spent some time questioning your thought process for the operation — your understanding of the picture and your intent. You know he's checking that the next generation is going to be at least as good as the last — and hopefully better; heritage is important to the Submarine Service. Teacher knows this too.

You're exhausted, and from the look of them, so are most of the crew. It's been an intense four weeks of pressure, externally and internally. All the 'assets' — the ships, submarines and helicopters trying to find *Triumph* in this game of 'cat and mouse' has sometimes been overwhelming. With very little downtime, you've managed to get just enough sleep on most days, and not enough on others. But here you are – the final phase.

"Ops Controller. Transmissions Bearing 190, classified 2089, helo in the Dip. Second set of transmissions bearing 260, classified 2089, second helo in the dip." The Sonar Controller says.

"All positions," you respond. "Duty Captain, hold reports, standby brief."

This is expected. The full ORBAT (Order of Battle) is out there and the two helicopters have been on task for an hour now.

"The focus is on avoiding counter-detection while continuing towards the objective. End of brief. Standard reports," you say over the intercom, almost without thinking. It's just natural now.

As the reports continue, one of the VIPs comes over to ask you another question. You're in the middle of answering when the general alarm sounds and ventilation is crash-stopped.

"Emergency Stations, Emergency Stations. Fire. Fire. Fire. Fire in the Weapon Storage Compartment."

You get out your Emergency Breathing System mask and put it on. This mask is really restrictive, you're breathing air in from an emergency system and exhaling which creates more noise. You have to shout to make yourself heard above the increased din and it's difficult to understand what people are saying through the mask. Every report is shouted and during an emergency, there are many of them. The civilian VIPs look on in awe at what looks like choreographed chaos. One of the Navy VIPs is explaining what's going on to them.

You listen intently. You're listening for things that are out of sequence or the report that's different from those you expect. You're also thinking 'What if?' What's the next thing that could happen and what will your response be? It's like chess, trying to think many moves ahead with a variety of options and it's what makes submarine operations so challenging.

The report comes in from the Damage Control Officer. They've operated the Weapons Storage Compartment spray. Should we abort or can we carry on? Should you push this position — two helicopters, two warships and now a fire which may render the weapons compartment temporarily out of action? You look over at the Ship Control Team.

"Ship Control, are you in control? Any issues?" you ask. The Ship Control Officer of the Watch replies that he's in control of the situation.

"What's your thinking Duty Captain?" one of the Admirals asks you.

"Sir, the team's in control of the situation. The helicopters are the greatest threat. The fire should get extinguished, but the atmosphere will be out of specification, so eventually, we're going to have to ventilate. That will probably be for an hour to get us off EBS and then we'll have to ventilate longer to return to normal. It's 30 minutes to get in and out and gather the intelligence. We can then go deep at speed and find somewhere to ventilate. That means we'll be on EBS for the next hour and a half. The intelligence is time sensitive and can have a strategic effect, so I'm going to continue with the mission."

The Admiral continues to ask questions and you answer them before picking up a bleep phone and giving the DCO the same brief. The DCO comes across on the main broadcast sharing this plan with the entire submarine.

"The fire is out. The fire is out. All compartments carry out atmosphere readings and report to DCHQ", comes across the main broadcast.

"Ops Controller, transmissions ceased. Helo Alfa and Helo Bravo are out of the dip."

Now is the time to move at speed, you decide.

"Officer of the Watch, take the submarine deep to 30 metres and come up in speed to 10 knots."

But before anything happens, the Captain intervenes. "Officer of the Watch, Captain. Belay that order. I have the submarine. Remain at periscope depth. Get DCHQ to end the exercise. Remove EBS in the Control Room. Prepare to surface. Duty Captain, you need to go below to the SINS compartment."

What's happened? What did you miss, you wonder. Is this the end? You take off your EBS and head down to the SINS compartment on 3 deck. As you do, you pass members of the Ship's Company stowing equipment, while others are preparing to get ready to surface.

Nobody looks at you, they're all focusing on what they need to do. You enter the tiny compartment, littered with planning charts and personal bags and sit down. You were doing okay, or so you thought. This is a weird feeling. You try to analyse where you may have made a bad decision or not led well enough. People fail this late on, that must be why the helicopters stopped transmitting – they're getting ready to take someone off. You try to curb your mounting sense of disappointment. But to have come this far…

Within five minutes you hear, "Surfacing now, surfacing now". You feel the boat shudder as air is pushed into the ballast tanks at 270 bar. She takes on a slight angle and then rests on the surface.

The submarine has been on the surface for five minutes when the other three students join you in the SINS Compartment. You look at each other. Everyone's thinking the same thing. Who's failed?

"Anyone hear anything? Do any of you know what's going on?" you ask. They all shake their heads. The door to the SINS compartment opens. It's the boat's Coxwain.

"Sir. Teacher would like to see you in the Wardroom."

You control your emotion. This is where you need your game face. As you go up the ladder from 3 deck to 2 deck, a few crewmembers glance at you as you pass by. It's been tough for them, putting this course on, and they'd already been away a long time on patrol before it began.

You head down a very narrow passageway towards the entrance to the Wardroom and knock on the door.

"Come in", Teacher says and you open it.

Teacher is standing there in front of you and around him are the VIPs and the Captain. As you approach him Teacher offers out his hand.

"Congratulations, Captain," he says and the rest clap. As the other students enter one by one, Teacher does the same with each. After you're all handed a glass of champagne, Teacher has some final words:

"Men, well done. You've demonstrated you can command a submarine. Your command-qualified journey begins now. Do well."

Appendix

Further Reading

The Art of War, Sun Tzu.
The Hard Thing about Hard Things, Ben Horowitz.
Leadership is an Art, Max de Pree.
Ethics, Aristotle.
Shackleton's Way, Margot Morrell & Stephanie Capparell.

Glossary

ARL	All-Round Look
ASW	Anti-Submarine Warfare
Attack BA	Fast Reaction Firefighting Team
CO	Commanding Officer
DC	Damage Control
DCO	Damage Control Officer
DCHQ	Damage Control Headquarters (also the wardroom)
EBS	Emergency Broadcast System
ECDIS	Electronic Chart System
FOST	Flag Officer Sea Training
GE	Garbage Ejector (Garbo)
GING	Fictional enemy simulated by NATO
HODs	Heads Of Department
HQ	Headquarters
HUMINT	Human Intelligence
ISTAR	Indication Surveillance Tracking and Reconnaissance
OOW	Officer of the Watch
ORBAT	Order of Battle
OST	Operational Sea Training
PD	Periscope Depth
POMA	Petty Officer Medical Assistant
SF	Special Forces
SINS	Ships Inertial Navigation Systems
SITREP	Situation Report
SMCC	Submarine Command Course
SME	Small and Medium Enterprises
SWOT	Strengths, Weaknesses, Opportunities and Threats
WECDIS	Warship Electronic Chart Display and Information System
WSC	Weapon Storage Compartment
W/T Room	Wireless Telegraphy Room
XO	Executive Officer

SUBMARINE CROSS-SECTION

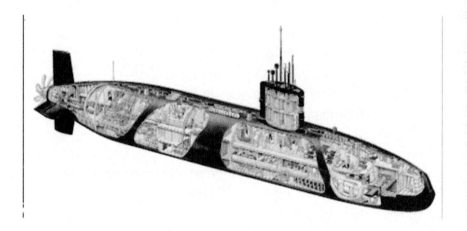

THE WALLIAN ARCHIPELAGO

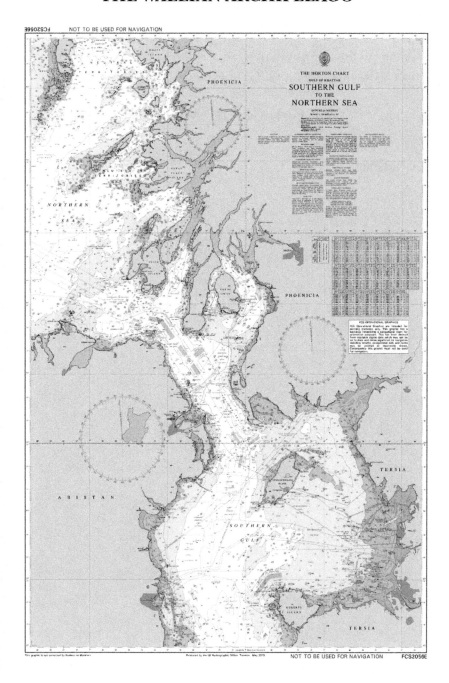

SEVEN QUESTIONS PLANNING TOOL

[To add: a completed example of the seven questions planning tool we used during pre-deployment training to prepare for combat against a fictional enemy — GING (simulated by NATO forces).]

LEADERSHIP MODEL

Leadership - simplified

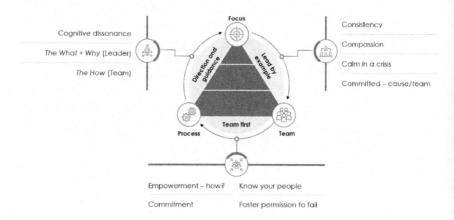

Notes

1. HMS Turbulent is the second Royal Navy submarine to bear the name. The first HMS Turbulent was a Triton Class submarine launched in 1941 which served during WW2 until 1943 when she was sunk by a mine close to the Maddalena Archipelago off Sardinia.
2. The Perisher scenarios used in this book are all taken from my time as Teacher. However, they are not in strict chronological order.
3. Martin MacPherson, Perisher: the making of a Submarine Commander in *100 Years of the Trade*, (CDISS, 2001).
4. Herman de Groot quoted in David Parry, *Perisher: 100 Years of the Submarine Command Course,* The Choir Press, 2022, p.12.
5. Carl Jung to Fanny Bowditch, 22 October 1916, in Carl Jung, Letters 1906-1950, Vol 1, Taylor & Francis, 2015.
6. In the 21st Century, this is less relevant because you need the sensors on the Search Periscope to achieve 'effect'. In the military 'effect' is used to mean having the desired effect on your enemy or potential enemy: to deter, disrupt, suppress or destroy.
7. Mike Guardia, *Hal Moore on Leadership: Winning when outgunned and outmanned,* Magnum Books, 2017, p.43.
8. ibid, p.100.
9. To keep it simple and show how you can apply this knowledge to business, I'm using the term 'micro expressions' to describe all facial expressions shorter than half a second. However, some of these micro expressions would, scientifically speaking, be more correctly identified as 'partial expressions', 'subtle expressions', or 'masked expressions'.
10. There are lots of books and courses to help you master this skill. Unmasking the Face, Paul Edkman, Wallace Friesen, Malor Books, 2003 explains how to correctly identify the seven basic emotions and how to tell when people are trying to mask or simulate them. It also has practical exercises to help you hone this skill.
11. Sun Tzu, *The Art of War,* Arcturus, 2020.
12. Adrian Groenewald *Seamless Leadership,* Jonathan Ball Publishers 2015, p184.

13. Sun Tzu, *The Art of War*, Arcturus, 2020.

14. See map in the appendix.

15. When asked by a reporter in 1997 if he was worried about Evander Holyfield's fight plan, Mike Tyson is said to have replied 'Everyone has a plan until they get punched in the mouth'.

16. TOPGUN's official name is the Navy Strike Fighter Tactics Instructor program or SFTI, for short.

17. This quote is most often credited to General George S. Patton, Jr. (1885-1945). He might well have said it during one of his famous speeches to his men before going into battle. However, Stanford University Professor Edward Krehbiel also used the phrase in 1919, before Patton became a public figure.

18. Ruth Murray-Webster & Darren Dalcher, *APM Body of Knowledge*, Association of Project Management, 7th edition, 2019.

19. Stockton Rush quoted in LBC article: 'I've broken some rules", June 2023. Available at: https://www.lbc.co.uk/news/ive-broken-some-rules-oceangate-titanic-submarine-window-pressure/. Accessed June 2023.

20. OceanGate employees quoted in BBC article 'Titanic sub firm: A maverick, rule-breaking founder and a tragic end. Available at: bbc.co.uk/news/world-us-canada-66014565. Accessed June 2023.

21. Stockton Rush quoted in BBC article 'Titanic sub firm: A maverick, rule-breaking founder and a tragic end. Available at: bbc.co.uk/news/world-us-canada-66014565. Accessed June 2023.

22. Stockton Rush to CBS reporter David Pogue, 2022. Interview available at: https://www.cbsnews.com/news/titanic-submersible-interview-transcript-with-oceangate-ceo-stockton-rush/ Accessed June 2023.

23. James Cameron quoted in National Geographic, available online at: https://www.nationalgeographic.com/science/article/exclusive-titan-exploration-james-cameron-bob-ballard?loggedin=true&rnd=1688118381769 Accessed June 2023.

24. John Harvey-Jones, *Making it Happen: Reflections on Leadership*, Harper Collins, 1988.

25. Merriam-Webster, online, accessed May 2023.

26. Ben Horowitz, *The Hard Thing about Hard Things*, Harper Collins, 2014, p.213.

27. Max de Pree, *Leadership is an Art*, Currency, 2004.

28. Jeff Conklin, *Dialogue Mapping: Building Shared Understanding of Wicked Problems*, Wiley, October 2005.

29. James Lovelock, *Novascene: The Coming of Age of Hyperintelligence*, Penguin, 2019, p.20.

30. Brett Crozier quoted in Seapower Magazine, available at: https:// seapowermagazine.org/decision-on-croziers-fate-in-the-hands-of-pentagon-officials/ accessed May 2023.

31. Adam Smith quoted in The Hill, available at: https://thehill.com/ policy/defense/navy/494553 accessed May 2023.

32. CBS News, 9 January 2020.

33. Adam Smith, *The Theory of Moral Sentiments*, Millar, 1759, p.4.

34. Frederique de Vignemont & Tania Singer, 'The Empathic Brain: How, When, and Why?', *Trends in Cognitive Sciences* 10, 2006, pp.435-41.

35. Leonard Mlodinow, *Emotional: The New Thinking About Feelings*, Penguin, 2022, p.187.

36. Marcus Aurelius and Gregory Hays, *Meditations: A New Translation*, Random House, 2002.

37. Mathew, D. Lieberman et al., 'Putting feelings into words', *Psychological Science* 18, 2007, pp. 421-428.

38. Jim Harter, Gallup Business Journal, 2023.

Printed in Great Britain
by Amazon

40060900R00126